Books by Willa Cather published by
the University of Nebraska Press

Alexander's Bridge

April Twilights, Revised Edition
ed. with an intro. by Bernice Slote

The Kingdom of Art:
Willa Cather's First Principles and Critical Statements, 1893–1896
selected and ed. with two essays and a commentary by Bernice Slote

My Ántonia
ed. by Charles Mignon and Kari Ronning

Not Under Forty

O Pioneers!
ed. by Susan J. Rosowski and Charles Mignon with Kathleen Danker

The Troll Garden: A Definitive Edition
ed. by James Woodress

Uncle Valentine and Other Stories:
Willa Cather's Uncollected Short Fiction, 1915–1929
ed. with an intro. by Bernice Slote

Willa Cather in Europe:
Her Own Story of the First Journey

Willa Cather in Person:
Interviews, Speeches, and Letters
ed. by L. Brent Bohlke

Willa Cather's Collected Short Fiction, 1892–1912
*Revised Edition ed. by Virginia Faulkner
with intro. by Mildred R. Bennett*

Willa Cather on Writing:
Critical Studies on Writing as an Art

Not Under Forty

BY

WILLA CATHER

University of Nebraska Press
Lincoln and London

First Bison Book printing: 1988
Most recent printing indicated by the first digit below:

       3   4   5   6   7   8   9   10

Library of Congress Cataloging-in-Publication Data
Cather, Willa, 1873–1947.
   Not under forty.
   "Bison"
   Reprint. Originally published: New York: A.A. Knopf, 1922.
   I. Title.
PS3505.A87N7   1988   814'.52   88-14282
ISBN 0-8032-6331-7 (pbk.)

Published by arrangement with Alfred A. Knopf, Inc.

∞

PREFATORY NOTE

The title of this book is meant to be " arresting "
only in the literal sense, like the signs put up
for motorists: " ROAD UNDER REPAIR," etc.
It means that the book will have little interest
for people under forty years of age. The world
broke in two in 1922 or thereabouts, and the persons and prejudices recalled in these sketches
slid back into yesterday's seven thousand years.
Thomas Mann, to be sure, belongs immensely to
the forward-goers, and they are concerned only
with his forwardness. But he also goes back a long
way, and his backwardness is more gratifying to
the backward. It is for the backward, and by one
of their number, that these sketches were written.

THE AUTHOR

CONTENTS

NOT UNDER FORTY

A CHANCE MEETING

I

It happened at Aix-les-Bains, one of the pleas-
antest places in the world. I was staying at the
Grand-Hôtel d'Aix, which opens on the sloping
little square with the bronze head of Queen Vic-
toria, commemorating her visits to that old water-
ing-place in Savoie. The Casino and the Opera
are next door, just across the gardens. The hotel
was built for the travellers of forty years ago, who
liked large rooms and large baths, and quiet. It is
not at all smart, but very comfortable. Long ago

I used to hear old Pittsburghers and Philadelphians talk of it. The newer hotels, set on the steep hills above the town, have the fashionable trade; the noise and jazz and dancing.

In the dining-room I often noticed, at a table not far from mine, an old lady, a Frenchwoman, who usually lunched and dined alone. She seemed very old indeed, well over eighty, and somewhat infirm, though not at all withered or shrunken. She was not stout, but her body had that rather shapeless heaviness which for some detestable reason often settles upon people in old age. The thing one especially noticed was her fine head, so well set upon her shoulders and beautiful in shape, recalling some of the portrait busts of Roman ladies. Her forehead was low and straight, her nose made just the right angle with it, and there was something quite lovely about her temples, something one very rarely sees.

As I watched her entering and leaving the dining-room I observed that she was slightly lame, and that she utterly disregarded it — walked with a quick, short step and great impatience, holding her shoulders well back. One saw that she was contemptuously intolerant of the limitations of old age. As she passed my table she often gave me a keen look and a half-smile (her eyes were extremely bright and clear), as if she were about to speak. But I remained blank. I am a poor linguist, and there would be no point in uttering commonplaces to this old lady; one knew that much about her, at a glance. If one spoke to her at all, one must be at ease.

Several times in the early morning I happened to see her leave the hotel in her motor, and each time her chauffeur brought down and placed in the car a camp chair, an easel, and canvases and colour boxes strapped together. Then they drove off toward the mountains. A plucky old lady, certainly, to go sketching in that very hot weather — for this was in the latter part of August 1930, one of the hottest seasons Aix-les-Bains had ever known. Every evening after dinner the old lady disappeared into the lift and went to her own rooms. But often she reappeared later, dressed for the opera, and went out, attended by her maid.

Not Under Forty

One evening, when there was no opera, I found her smoking a cigarette in the lounge, where I had gone to write letters. It was a very hot night, and all the windows were open; seeing her pull her lace shawl closer about her shoulders, I went to shut one of them. Then she spoke to me in excellent English: —

"I think that draught blows out from the dining-room. If you will ask the boy to close the doors, we shall not feel the air."

I found the boy and had the doors closed. When I returned, the old lady thanked me, motioned to a chair at her side, and asked if I had time for a cigarette.

"You are stopping at Aix for some time, I judge?" she asked as I sat down.

I replied that I was.

"You like it, then? You are taking a cure? You have been here before?"

No, I was not taking a cure. I had been here before, and had come back merely because I liked the place.

A Chance Meeting

" It has changed less than most places, I think,"
she remarked. " I have been coming here for
thirty-five years; I have old associations with Aix-
les-Bains. Besides, I enjoy the music here. I live in
the South, at Antibes. You attend the Grand-
Cercle? You heard the performance of *Tristan
and Iseult* last night? "

I had not heard it. I told her I had thought the
evening too frightfully hot to sit in a theatre.

" But it was no hotter there than anywhere else.
I was not uncomfortable."

There was a reprimand in her tone, and I added
the further excuse that I had thought the princi-
pals would probably not be very good, and that I
liked to hear that opera well sung.

" They were well enough," she declared.
" With Wagner I do not so much care about the
voices. It is the orchestra I go to hear. The conductor last night was Albert Wolff, one of our
best *Kapellmeister*."

I said I was sorry I had missed the opera.

" Are you going to his classical concert tomorrow afternoon? He will give a superb rendering of Ravel's *La Valse* — if you care for modern music."

I hastily said that I meant to go.

" But have you reserved your places? No? Then I would advise you to do so at once. The best way here is to have places for the entire chain of performances. One need not go to all, of course; but it is the best way. There is little else to do here in the evening, unless one plays at the gaming tables. Besides, it is almost September; the days are lowering now, and one needs the theatre." The old lady stopped, frowned, and made an impatient gesture with her very interesting hand. " What should I have said then? Lowering is not the word, but I seldom have opportunity to speak English."

" You might say the days are growing shorter, but I think lowering a very good word."

" *Mais un peu poétique, n'est-ce pas?* "

" Perhaps; but it is the right kind of poetic."

" And by that you mean? "

" That it's not altogether bookish or literary. The country people use it in some parts of England, I think. I have heard old-fashioned farmers use it in America, in the South."

The old lady gave a dry little laugh. " So if the farmers use a word it is quite safe, eh? "

Yes, I told her, that was exactly what I meant; safe.

We talked a little longer on that first occasion. She asked if I had been to Chamonix, and strongly advised me to go to a place near Sallanches, where she had lately been visiting friends, on her way to Aix-les-Bains. In replying to her questions I fell into the stupid way one sometimes adopts when speaking to people of another language; tried to explain something in very simple words. She frowned and checked me with: " Speak idiomatically, please. I knew English quite well at one time. If I speak it badly, it is because now I have no practice."

I said good-night and sat down at a desk to write letters. But on the way to my room I stopped to tell the friend with whom I was travelling that the old French lady we had so often admired spoke very good English, and spoke it easily; that she seemed, indeed, to have a rather special feeling for language.

II

The next day was intensely hot. In the morning the beautiful mountain ridges which surround Aix stood out sharp and clear, but the vineyards looked wilted. Toward noon the hills grew misty, and the sun poured down through a slightly milky atmosphere. I rather dreaded the heat of a concert hall, but at two o'clock I went to Albert Wolff's concert, and heard such a rendition of Ravel's *La Valse* as I do not expect to hear again; a small orchestra, wonderfully trained, and a masterly conductor.

The program was long, with two intermissions. The last group did not seem to be especially interesting, and the concert was quite long enough, and fine enough, without those numbers. I decided that I could miss them. I would go up to the Square and have tea beside the Roman arch. As I left the hall by the garden entrance, I saw the old French lady seated on the veranda with her maid, wearing a white dress and a white lace garden hat, fanning herself vigorously, the beads of moisture on her face making dark streaks in the powder. She beckoned to me and asked whether I had enjoyed the music. I told her that I had, very much indeed; but now my capacity for enjoying, or even listening, was quite spent, and I was going up to the Square for tea.

"Oh, no," said she, "that is not necessary. You can have your tea here at the Maison des Fleurs quite well, and still have time to go back for the last group."

I thanked her and went across the garden, but I did not mean to see the concert through. Seeing things through was evidently a habit with this old lady: witness the way she was seeing life through, going to concerts and operas in this wilting heat; being concerned that other people should go, moreover, and caring about the way in which Ravel was played, when in the course of nature her interest in new music should have stopped with César Franck, surely.

I left the Casino gardens through a grotto that

gave into the street, went up to the Square, and had tea with some nice English people I had met on Mont Revard, a young business man and his wife come over for their holiday. I felt a little as if I had escaped from an exacting preceptress. The old lady took it for granted that one wished to accomplish as much as possible in a given space of time. I soon found that, to her, life meant just that — accomplishing things; " doing them always a little better and better," as she once remarked after I came to know her.

While I was dressing for dinner I decided to go away for a few days, up into the high mountains of Haute-Savoie, under Mont Blanc. That evening, when the old lady stopped me to discuss the concert, I asked her for some suggestions about the hotels there, since at our first meeting she had said I must certainly go to some of the mountain places easily reached from Sallanches.

She at once recommended a hotel that was very high and cool, and then told me of all the excursions I must make from that place, outlining a full program which I knew I should not follow. I was going away merely to escape the heat and to regard Mont Blanc from an advantageous point — not to become acquainted with the country.

III

My trip into the mountains was wholly successful. All the suggestions the old lady had given me proved excellent, and I felt very grateful to her. I stayed away longer than I had intended. I returned to Aix-les-Bains late one night, got up early the next morning, and went to the bank, feeling that Aix is always a good place to come back to. When I returned to the hotel for lunch, there was the old lady, sitting in a chair just outside the door, looking worn and faded. Why, since she had her car and her driver there, she had not run away from the heat, I do not know. But she had stayed through it, and gone out sketching every morning. She greeted me very cordially, asked whether I had an engagement for the evening, and suggested that we should meet in the salon after dinner.

I was dining with my friend, and after dinner

we both went into the writing-room where the old lady was awaiting us. Our acquaintance seemed to have progressed measurably in my absence, though neither of us as yet knew the other's name. Her name, I thought, would mean very little; she was what she was. No one could fail to recognize her distinction and authority; it was in the carriage of her head, in her fine hands, in her voice, in every word she uttered in any language, in her brilliant, very piercing eyes. I had no curiosity about her name; that would be an accident and could scarcely matter.

We talked very comfortably for a time. The old lady made some comment on the Soviet experiment in Russia. My friend remarked that it was fortunate for the great group of Russian writers that none of them had lived to see the Revolution; Gogol, Tolstoi, Turgeniev.

" Ah, yes," said the old lady with a sigh, " for Turgeniev, especially, all this would have been very terrible. I knew him well at one time."

I looked at her in astonishment. Yes, of course,

A Chance Meeting

it was possible. She was very old. I told her I had never met anyone who had known Turgeniev.

She smiled. " No? I saw him very often when I was a young girl. I was much interested in German, in the great works. I was making a translation of *Faust*, for my own pleasure, merely, and Turgeniev used to go over my translation and correct it from time to time. He was a great friend of my uncle. I was brought up in my uncle's house." She was becoming excited as she spoke, her face grew more animated, her voice warmer, something flashed in her eyes, some strong feeling awoke in her. As she went on, her voice shook a little. " My mother died at my birth, and I was brought up in my uncle's house. He was more than father to me. My uncle also was a man of letters, Gustave Flaubert, you may perhaps know . . ." She murmured the last phrase in a curious tone, as if she had said something indiscreet and were evasively dismissing it.

The meaning of her words came through to me slowly; so this must be the " Caro " of the *Lettres à sa Nièce Caroline.* There was nothing to say, certainly. The room was absolutely quiet, but there was nothing to say to this disclosure. It was like being suddenly brought up against a mountain of memories. One could not see round it; one could only stupidly realize that in this mountain which the old lady had conjured up by a phrase and a name or two lay most of one's mental past. Some moments went by. There was no word with which one could greet such a revelation. I took one of her lovely hands and kissed it, in homage to a great period, to the names that made her voice tremble.

She laughed an embarrassed laugh, and spoke hurriedly. " Oh, that is not necessary! That is not at all necessary." But the tone of distrust, the faint challenge in that " you may perhaps know . . ." had disappeared. " *Vous connaissez bien les œuvres de mon oncle?* "

Who did not know them? I asked her.

Again the dry tone, with a shrug. " Oh, I almost never meet anyone who really knows them. The name, of course, its place in our literature, but not the works themselves. I never meet anyone now who cares much about them."

Great names are awkward things in conversation, when one is a chance acquaintance. One cannot be too free with them; they have too much value. The right course, I thought, was to volunteer nothing, above all to ask no questions; to let the old lady say what she would, ask what she would. She wished, it seemed, to talk about *les œuvres de mon oncle*. Her attack was uncertain; she touched here and there. It was a large subject. She told me she had edited the incomplete *Bouvard et Pécuchet* after his death, that *La Tentation de Saint Antoine* had been his own favourite among his works; she supposed I would scarcely agree with his choice?

No, I was sorry, but I could not.

" I suppose you care most for *Madame Bovary?* "

One can hardly discuss that book; it is a fact in history. One knows it too well to know it well.

" And yet," she murmured, " my uncle got only five hundred francs for it from the publisher. Of course, he did not write for money. Still, he would have been pleased . . . Which one, then, do you prefer? "

I told her that a few years ago I had reread *L'Éducation sentimentale*, and felt that I had never risen to its greatness before.

She shook her head. " Ah, too long, prolix, *trop de conversation*. And Frédéric is very weak."

But there was an eagerness in her face, and I knew by something in her voice that this was like Garibaldi's proclamation to his soldiers on the retreat from Rome, when he told them he could offer them cold and hunger and sickness and misery. He offered something else, too, but the listeners must know that for themselves.

It had seemed to me when I last read *L'Éducation sentimentale* that its very faults were of a noble kind. It is too cold, certainly, to justify the subtitle, *Roman d'un jeune homme;* for youth, even when it has not generous enthusiasm, has at least fierce egotism. But I had wondered whether this cool, dispassionate, almost contemptuous presentation of Frédéric were not a protest against the overly sympathetic manner of Balzac in his stories of young men: Eugène de Rastignac, Lucien de Rubempré, Horace Bianchon, and all the others. Certainly Balzac's habit of playing up his characters, of getting into the ring and struggling and sweating with them, backing them with all his animal heat, must have been very distasteful to Flaubert. It was perhaps this quality of salesmanship in Balzac which made Flaubert say of him in a letter to this same niece Caroline: " He is as ignorant as a pot, and bourgeois to the marrow."

Of course, a story of youth, which altogether lacks that gustatory zest, that exaggerated concern for trivialities, is scarcely successful. In *L'Éducation* the trivialities are there (for life is made up of them), but not the voracious appetite which drives young people through silly and vulgar experiences. The story of Frédéric is a story of youth with the heart of youth left out; and of course it is often dull. But the latter chapters of the book justify one's journey through it. Then all the hero's young life becomes more real than it was as one followed it from year to year, and the story ends on a high plateau. From that great and quiet last scene, seated by the fire with the two middle-aged friends (who were never really friends, but who had been young together), one looks back over Frédéric's life and finds that one has it all, even the dull stretches. It is something one has lived through, not a story one has read; less diverting than a story, perhaps, but more inevitable. One is " left with it," in the same way that one is left with a weak heart after certain illnesses. A shadow has come into one's consciousness that will not go out again.

The old French lady and I talked for some time about *L'Éducation sentimentale*. She spoke with warm affection, with tenderness, of Madame Arnoux.

" Ah yes, Madame Arnoux, she is beautiful! " The moisture in her bright eyes, the flush on her cheeks, and the general softening of her face said much more. That charming and good woman of the middle classes, the wife who holds the story together (as she held Frédéric himself together), passed through the old lady's mind so vividly that it was as if she had entered the room. Madame Arnoux was there with us, in that hotel at Aix, on the evening of September 5, 1930, a physical presence, in the charming costume of her time, as on the night when Frédéric first dined at 24 rue de Choiseul. The niece had a very special feeling for this one of her uncle's characters. She lingered over the memory, recalling her as she first appears, sitting on the bench of a passenger boat on the Seine, in her muslin gown sprigged with green and her wide straw hat with red ribbons. Whenever the old lady mentioned Madame Arnoux it was with some mark of affection; she smiled, or sighed, or shook her head as we do when we speak of something that is quite unaccountably fine: " Ah yes, she is lovely, Madame Arnoux! She is very complete."

The old lady told me that she had at home the corrected manuscript of *L'Éducation sentimentale*. " Of course I have many others. But this he gave me long before his death. You shall see it when you come to my place at Antibes.

I call my place the Villa Tanit, *pour la déesse,*"
she added with a smile.

The name of the goddess took us back to
Salammbô, which is the book of Flaubert I like
best. I like him in those great reconstructions of
the remote and cruel past. When I happened to
speak of the splendid final sentence of *Hérodias,*
where the fall of the syllables is so suggestive of
the hurrying footsteps of John's disciples, carrying away with them their prophet's severed head,
she repeated that sentence softly: "*Comme elle
était très lourde, ils la portaient al-ter-na-tiv-e-
ment.*"

The hour grew late. The maid had been standing in the corridor a long while, waiting for her
mistress. At last the old lady rose and drew her
wrap about her.

"Good night, madame. May you have pleasant dreams. As for me, I shall not sleep; you have
recalled too much." She went toward the lift
with the energetic, unconquered step with which
she always crossed the dining-room, carrying

with hardihood a body no longer perfectly under her control.

When I reached my room and opened my windows I, too, felt that sleep was far from me. The full moon (like the moon in *Salammbô*) stood over the little square and flooded the gardens and quiet streets and the misty mountains with light. The old lady had brought that great period of French letters very near; a period which has meant so much in the personal life of everyone to whom French literature has meant anything at all.

IV

Probably all those of us who had the good fortune to come upon the French masters accidentally, and not under the chilling guidance of an instructor, went through very much the same experience. We all began, of course, with Balzac. And to young people, for very good reasons, he seems the final word. They read and reread him, and live in his world; to inexperience, that world is neither overpeopled nor overfurnished. When they begin to read Flaubert — usually *Madame Bovary* is the introduction — they resent the change of tone; they miss the glow, the ardour, the temperament. (It is scarcely exaggeration to say that if one is not a little mad about Balzac at twenty, one will never live; and if at forty one can still take Rastignac and Lucien de Rubempré at Balzac's own estimate, one has lived in vain.) We first read *Bovary* with a certain hostility; the wine is too dry for us. We try, perhaps, another work of Flaubert, and with a shrug go back to Balzac. But young people who are at all sensitive to certain qualities in writing will not find the Balzac they left. Something has happened to them which dampens their enjoyment. For a time it looks as if they had lost both Balzac and Flaubert. They recover both, eventually, and read each for what he is, having learned that an artist's limitations are quite as important as his powers; that they are a definite asset, not a deficiency, and that both go to form his flavour, his personality, the thing by which the ear can immediately recognize Flaubert, Stendhal, Méri-mée, Thomas Hardy, Conrad, Brahms, César Franck.

The fact remains that Balzac, like Dickens and Scott, has a strong appeal for the great multitudes of humanity who have no feeling for any form of art, and who read him only in poor translations. This is overwhelming evidence of the vital force in him, which no rough handling can diminish. Also it implies the lack in him of certain qualities which matter to only a few people, but matter very much. The time in one's life when one first began to sense the things which Flaubert stood for, to admire (almost against one's will) that peculiar integrity of language and vision, that coldness which, in him, is somehow noble — that is a pleasant chapter of one's life to remember, and Madame Franklin Grout had brought it back within arm's length of me that night.

V

For that was her name. Next morning the *valet de chambre* brought me a visiting card on which was engraved:

MADAME FRANKLIN GROUT

ANTIBES

In one corner *Villa Tanit* was written in purple ink.

In the evening we sat in the writing-room again, and Madame Grout's talk touched upon many things. On the Franco-Prussian War, for instance, and its effect upon her uncle. He had seen to it that she herself was comfortably settled in England through most of that troubled time. And during the late war of 1914 she had been in Italy a great deal. She loved Italian best of all the languages she spoke so well. (She spoke Swedish, even; she had lived for a time in Sweden during the life of her first husband, who had business interests there.)

She talked of Turgeniev, of her uncle's affection for him and great admiration for him as an artist.[1] She liked to recall his pleasant visits to Croisset, which were the reward of long anticipation on the part of the hosts. Turgeniev usually fixed the date by letter, changed it by another letter, then again by telegram — and sometimes he did not come at all. Flaubert's mother prepared for these visits by inspecting all the beds in the house, but she never found one long enough to hold " le Moscove " comfortably.

Madame Grout seemed to remember with especial pleasure the evenings when he used to sit at the table with her, going over her translation of *Faust:* " That noble man, to give his time

[1] Madame Grout's regard for Turgeniev seems to have been warmly returned. In a letter written to her in 1873, immediately after one of Turgeniev's visits to Croisset, Flaubert says: " Mon Moscove m'a quitté ce matin. . . . Tu l'as tout à fait séduit, mon loulou! car à plusieurs reprises il m'a parlé de ' mon adorable nièce,' de ' ma charmante nièce,' ' ravissante femme,' etc., etc. Enfin le Moscove t'adore! ce qui me fait bien plaisir, car c'est un homme exquis. Tu ne t'imagines pas ce qu'il sait! Il m'a répété, par cœur, des morceaux des tragédies de Voltaire, et de Luce de Lancival! Il connaît, je crois, *toutes* les littératures jusque dans leurs bas-fonds! Et si modeste avec tout cela! si bonhomme! si *vache!* "

to my childish efforts! " She well remembered
the period during which he was writing *Les Eaux
printanières*, and her own excitement when she
first read that work. Like Henry James, she
seemed to resent Turgeniev's position in the
Viardot household; recalling it, even after such a
long stretch of time, with vexation. " And when
they gave a hunt, he looked after the dogs! " she
murmured under her breath. She talked one evening of his sad latter years: of his disappointment
in his daughter, of his long and painful illness, of
the way in which the death of his friends, going
one after another, contracted his life and made
it bleak. But these were very personal memories,
and if Madame Grout had wished to make them
public, she would have written them herself.

Madame Viardot she had known very well,
and for many years after Turgeniev's death.
" Pauline Viardot was a superb artist, very intelligent and engaging as a woman, with a great
charm — and, *au fond*, very Spanish! " she said.
Of Monsieur Louis Viardot she did not think
highly. I gathered that he was agreeable, but not

much more than that. When I asked her whether Monsieur Viardot had not translated some of Turgeniev's books into French, the old lady lifted her brows and there was a mocking glint in her eyes.

" Turgeniev himself translated them; Viardot may have looked over his shoulder! "

George Sand she did not like. Yes, she readily admitted, her men friends were very loyal to her, had a great regard for her; *mon oncle* valued her comradeship; but Madame Grout found the lady's personality distasteful.

I gathered that, for Madame Grout, George Sand did not really fill any of the great rôles she assigned herself: the devoted mistress, the staunch comrade and " good fellow," the self-sacrificing mother. George Sand's men friends believed her to be all these things; and certainly she herself believed that she was. But Madame Grout seemed to feel that in these various relations Madame Dudevant was self-satisfied rather than self-forgetful; always self-admiring and a trifle unctuous. Madame Grout's distaste for this baffling kind of falseness was immediate and instinctive — it put her teeth on edge. Turgeniev, that penetrating reader of women, seems never to have felt this shallowness in his friend. But in Chopin's later letters one finds that he, to his bitter cost, had become aware of it — curiously enough, through Madame Dudevant's behaviour toward her own children! It is clear that he had come upon something so subtly false, so excruciatingly aslant, that when he briefly refers to it his sentences seem to shudder.

Though I tried to let Madame Grout direct our conversations without suggestion from me, and never to question her, I did ask her whether she read Marcel Proust with pleasure.

"*Trop dur et trop fatigant,*" she murmured, and dismissed the greatest French writer of his time with a wave of her hand.

When I made some reference to Anatole France she said quickly: "Oh, I like him very much! But I like him most where he is most indebted to my uncle!"

When she was tired, or deeply moved,

A Chance Meeting

Madame Grout usually spoke French; but when she spoke English it was as flexible as it was correct. She spoke like an Englishwoman, with no French accent at all.

What astonished me in her was her keen and sympathetic interest in modern music; in Ravel, Scriabin, Albéniz, Stravinsky, De Falla. Only a few days before I quitted Aix I found her at the box office in person, getting exactly the seats she wanted for a performance of *Boris Godounov*. She must change her habitual seat, as she had asked some friends to come over from Sallanches to hear the opera with her. " You will certainly hear it? Albert Wolff is conducting for the last time this season, and he does it very well," she explained.

It was interesting to observe Madame Grout at the opera that night, to watch the changes that went over her face as she listened with an attention that never wandered, looking younger and stronger than she ever did by day, as if the music were some very potent stimulant. Any form of pleasure, I had noticed, made her keener,

more direct and positive, more authoritative, re-
vived in her the stamp of a period which had
achieved a great style in art. In a letter which
Flaubert wrote her when she was a young
woman, he said: —

> " C'est une joie profonde pour moi, mon
> pauvre loulou, que de t'avoir donné le goût des
> occupations intellectuelles. Que d'ennuis et de
> sottises il vous épargne! "

Certainly those interests had stood her in
good stead, and for many more years than the
uncle himself lived through. She had still, at
eighty-four, a capacity for pleasure such as very
few people in this world ever know at all.

VI

The next morning I told Madame Grout that,
because of the illness of a friend, I must start at
once for Paris.

And when, she asked, could I return and go
south to Antibes and the Villa Tanit, to see her
Flaubert collection, and the interior of his study,

A Chance Meeting

which she had brought down there thirty-five years ago?

I told her I was afraid that visit must be put off until next summer.

She gave a very charming laugh. " At my age, of course, the future is somewhat uncertain! " Then she asked whether, on her return to Antibes, she could send me some souvenir of our meeting; would I like to have something that had belonged to her uncle, or some letter written by him?

I told her that I was not a collector; that manuscripts and autographed letters meant very little to me. The things of her uncle that were valuable to me I already had, and had had for years. It rather hurt me that she should think I wanted any material reminder of her or of Flaubert. It was the Flaubert in her mind and heart that was to give me a beautiful memory.

On the following day, at *déjeuner*, I said goodbye to Madame Grout; I was leaving on the two o'clock train. It was a hurried and mournful parting, but there was real feeling on both sides.

She had counted upon my staying longer, she said. But she did not for a moment take on a slightly aggrieved tone, as many privileged old ladies would have done. There was nothing " wayward " or self-indulgent about Madame Grout; the whole discipline of her life had been to the contrary. One had one's objective, and one went toward it; one had one's duty, and one did it as best one could.

The last glimpse I had of her was as she stood in the dining-room, the powder on her face quite destroyed by tears, her features agitated, but her head erect and her eyes flashing. And the last words I heard from her expressed a hope that I would always remember the pleasure we had had together in talking unreservedly about *les œuvres de mon oncle*. Standing there, she seemed holding to that name as to a staff. A great memory and a great devotion were the things she lived upon, certainly; they were her armour against a world concerned with insignificant matters.

A Chance Meeting

VII

When I got back to Paris and began to re-read the *Lettres de Flaubert à sa Nièce Caroline*, I found that the personality of Madame Grout sent a wonderful glow over the pages. I was now almost startled (in those letters written her when she was still a child) by his solicitude about her progress in her English lessons — those lessons by which I was to profit seventy-three years afterward!

The five hundred pages of that book were now peopled for me with familiar figures, like the chronicles of a family I myself had known. It will always be for me one of the most delightful of books; and in none of his letters to other correspondents does Gustave Flaubert himself seem so attractive.

In reading over those letters, covering a stretch of twenty-four years, with the figure of Madame Grout in one's mind, one feels a kind of happiness and contentment about the whole situation — yes, and gratitude to Fate! The great man might have written very charming and ten-

der and warmly confidential letters to a niece
who was selfish, vain, intelligent merely in a
conventional way — because she was the best he
had! One can never be sure about such things; a
heartless and stupid woman may be so well educated, after all!

But having known Madame Grout, I know
that she had the root of the matter in her; that
no one could be more sensitive than she to all
that was finest in Flaubert's work, or more quick
to admit the qualities he did not have — which
is quite as important.

During all his best working years he had in
his house beside him, or within convenient distance for correspondence, one of his own blood,
younger and more ardent than he, who absolutely
understood what he was doing; who could feel
the great qualities of his failures, even. Could
any situation be happier for a man of letters?
How many writers have found one understanding ear among their sons or daughters?

Moreover, Caroline was the daughter of a
sister whom Flaubert had devotedly loved. He

took her when she was an infant into his house at Croisset, where he lived alone with his old mother. What delight for a solitary man of letters and an old lady to have a baby to take care of, the little daughter of a beloved daughter! They had all the pleasure of her little girlhood — and she must have been an irresistible little girl! Flaubert spent a great deal of time attending to her early education, and when he was seated at his big writing-table, or working in bed, he liked to have her in the room, lying on a rug in the corner with her book. For hours she would not speak, she told me; she was so passionately proud of the fact that he wanted her to be there. When she was just beginning to read, she liked to think, as she lay in her corner, that she was shut in a cage with some powerful wild animal, a tiger or a lion or a bear, who had devoured his keeper and would spring upon anyone else who opened his door, but with whom she was " quite safe and conceited," as she said with a chuckle.

During his short stays in Paris, Flaubert writes

to Caroline about her favourite rabbit, and the imaginary characters with whom she had peopled the garden at Croisset. He sends his greetings to Caroline's doll, Madame Robert: —

" Remercie de ma part Mme. Robert qui a bien voulu se rappeler de moi. Présente-lui mes respects et conseille-lui un régime fortifiant, car elle me paraît un peu pale, et je ne suis pas sans inquiétude sur sa santé."

In a letter from Paris, dated just a year later, when Caroline was eleven, he tells her that he is sending her Thierry's *Récits des temps mérovingiens*, and adds: —

" Je suis bien aise que les *Récits mérovingiens* t'amusent; relis-les quand tu auras fini; *apprends des dates*, tu as tes programmes, et passe tous les jours quelque temps à regarder une carte de géographie."

One sees from the letters with what satisfaction Flaubert followed every step of Caroline's development. Her facility in languages was a matter of the greatest pride to him, though even after she is married and living abroad he occasionally finds fault with her orthography: —

"Un peu d'orthographe ne te nuirait pas, mon bibi! car tu écris *aplomb* par deux *p:* 'Moral et physique sont d'applomb,' trois *p* marqueraient encore plus d'énergie! Ça m'a amusé, parce que ça te ressemble."

Yes, it was like her, certainly; like her as she walked across the floor of that hotel dining-room in Aix-les-Bains, so many years afterward.

Though she had been married twice, Madame Grout, in our conversations, did not talk of either of her husbands. Her uncle had always been the great figure in her life, and even a short acquaintance with her made me feel that she possessed every quality for comradeship with him. Besides her devotion to him, her many gifts, her very unusual intelligence and intuition in art, she had moral qualities which he must have loved: poise, great good sense, and a love of fairness and justice. She had the habit of searching out facts and weighing evidence, for her own satisfaction. Her speech, when she was explaining something, had the qualities of good Latin prose: economy, elegance, and exactness. She was not an idealist; she had lived through two wars. She was one of the least visionary and sentimental persons I have ever met. She knew that conditions and circumstances, not their own wishes, dictate the actions of men. In her mind there was a kind of large enlightenment, like that of the many-windowed workroom at Crois-set, with the cool, tempered northern light pouring into it. In her, Flaubert had not only a companion, but a " daughter of the house " to cherish and protect. And he had her all his life, until the short seizure which took him off in an hour. And she, all her life, kept the handkerchief with which they had wiped the moisture from his brow a few moments before he died.

VIII

I sailed for Quebec in October. In November, while I was at Jaffrey, New Hampshire, a letter came from Madame Grout; the envelope had been opened and almost destroyed. I have received letters from Borneo and Java that looked much less travel-worn. She had addressed it to me in care of an obscure bookseller, on a small street in Paris, from whom she had got one of my books. (I suppose, in her day, all booksellers were publishers.) The letter had been forwarded through three publishing houses, and a part of its contents had got lost. In her letter Madame Grout writes that she is sending me " ci-joint une lettre de mon oncle Gustave Flaubert adressée à George Sand — elle doit être, je crois, de 1866. Il me semble qu'elle vous fera plaisir et j'ai plaisir à vous l'envoyer."

This enclosure had been removed. I regretted its loss chiefly because I feared it would distress Madame Grout. But I wrote her, quite truthfully, that her wish that I should have one of her uncle's letters meant a great deal more to me than the actual possession of it could mean. Nevertheless, it was an awkward explanation to make, and I delayed writing it until late in December. I did not hear from her again.

In February my friends in Paris sent me a clipping from the *Journal des Débats* which read: —

MORT DE MME. FRANKLIN-GROUT

Nous apprenons avec tristesse la mort de Mme. Franklin-Grout, qui s'est éteinte à Antibes, à la suite d'une courte maladie. Nièce de Gustave Flaubert, Mme. Franklin-Grout a joué un rôle important dans la diffusion et le succès des œuvres de son oncle. Exécutrice testamentaire du grand romancier, qui l'avait élevée et instruite, Mme. Franklin-Grout a publié la correspondance de son oncle, si précieuse pour sa psychologie littéraire, et qui nous a révélé les doctrines de Flaubert et sa vie de travail acharné. Mme. Franklin-Grout publia aussi *Bouvard et Pécuchet*. . . . Mme. Franklin-Grout était une personne charmante et distinguée, très attachée à ses amis et qui, jusqu'à la plus extrême vieillesse, avait conservé l'intelligence et la bonté souriante d'une spirituelle femme du monde.

THE NOVEL DÉMEUBLÉ

The novel, for a long while, has been over-furnished. The property-man has been so busy on its pages, the importance of material objects and their vivid presentation have been so stressed, that we take it for granted whoever can observe, and can write the English language, can write a novel. Often the latter qualification is considered unnecessary.

In any discussion of the novel, one must make it clear whether one is talking about the novel as a form of amusement, or as a form of art; since they serve very different purposes and in very different ways. One does not wish the egg one eats for breakfast, or the morning paper, to be made of the stuff of immortality. The novel manufactured to entertain great multitudes of people must be considered exactly like a cheap soap or a cheap perfume, or cheap furniture. Fine quality is a distinct disadvantage in articles made for great numbers of people who do not want quality but quantity, who do not want a thing that "wears," but who want change, — a succession of new things that are quickly threadbare and can be lightly thrown away. Does anyone pretend that if the Woolworth store windows were piled high with Tanagra figurines at ten cents, they could for a moment compete with Kewpie brides in the popular esteem? Amusement is one thing; enjoyment of art is another.

Every writer who is an artist knows that his "power of observation," and his "power of description," form but a low part of his equipment. He must have both, to be sure; but he knows that the most trivial of writers often have a very good observation. Mérimée said in his remarkable essay on Gogol: " L'art de choisir parmi les innombrable traits que nous offre la nature est, après tout, bien plus difficile que celui de les observer avec attention et de les rendre avec exactitude."

There is a popular superstition that " realism " asserts itself in the cataloguing of a great number of material objects, in explaining mechanical processes, the methods of operating manufactories and trades, and in minutely and unsparingly describing physical sensations. But is not realism, more than it is anything else, an attitude of mind on the part of the writer toward his material, a vague indication of the sympathy and candour with which he accepts, rather than chooses, his theme? Is the story of a banker who is unfaithful to his wife and who ruins himself by speculation in trying to gratify the caprices of his mistresses, at all reinforced by a masterly exposition of banking, our whole system of credits, the methods of the Stock Exchange? Of course, if the story is thin, these things do reinforce it in a sense, — any amount of red meat thrown into the scale to make the beam dip. But are the banking system and the Stock Exchange worth being written about at all? Have such things any proper place in imaginative art?

The automatic reply to this question is the name of Balzac. Yes, certainly, Balzac tried out the value of literalness in the novel, tried it out to the uttermost, as Wagner did the value of scenic literalness in the music drama. He tried it, too, with the passion of discovery, with the inflamed zest of an unexampled curiosity. If the heat of that furnace could not give hardness and sharpness to material accessories, no other brain will ever do it. To reproduce on paper the actual city of Paris; the houses, the upholstery, the food, the wines, the game of pleasure, the game of business, the game of finance: a stupendous ambition — but, after all, unworthy of an artist. In exactly so far as he succeeded in pouring out on his pages that mass of brick and mortar and

The Novel Démeublé

furniture and proceedings in bankruptcy, in exactly so far he defeated his end. The things by which he still lives, the types of greed and avarice and ambition and vanity and lost innocence of heart which he created — are as vital today as they were then. But their material surroundings, upon which he expended such labour and pains . . . the eye glides over them. We have had too much of the interior decorator and the " romance of business " since his day. The city he built on paper is already crumbling. Stevenson said he wanted to blue-pencil a great deal of Balzac's " presentation " — and he loved him beyond all modern novelists. But where is the man who could cut one sentence from the stories of Mérimée? And who wants any more detail as to how Carmencita and her fellow factory-girls made cigars? Another sort of novel? Truly. Isn't it a better sort?

In this discussion another great name naturally occurs. Tolstoi was almost as great a lover of material things as Balzac, almost as much interested in the way dishes were cooked, and people were dressed, and houses were furnished. But there is this determining difference: the clothes, the dishes, the haunting interiors of those old Moscow houses, are always so much a part of the emotions of the people that they are perfectly synthesized; they seem to exist, not so much in the author's mind, as in the emotional penumbra of the characters themselves. When it is fused like this, literalness ceases to be literalness — it is merely part of the experience.

If the novel is a form of imaginative art, it cannot be at the same time a vivid and brilliant form of journalism. Out of the teeming, gleaming stream of the present it must select the eternal material of art. There are hopeful signs that some of the younger writers are trying to break away from mere verisimilitude, and, following the development of modern painting, to interpret imaginatively the material and social investiture of their characters; to present their scene by suggestion rather than by enumeration. The higher processes of art are all processes of simplification. The novelist must learn to write, and then he must unlearn it; just as the modern painter learns to draw, and then learns when utterly to disregard his accomplishment, when to subordinate it to a higher and truer effect. In this direction only, it seems to me, can the novel develop into anything more varied and perfect than all the many novels that have gone before.

One of the very earliest American romances might well serve as a suggestion to later writers. In *The Scarlet Letter* how truly in the spirit of art is the mise-en-scène presented. That drudge, the theme-writing high-school student, could scarcely be sent there for information regarding the manners and dress and interiors of Puritan society. The material investiture of the story is presented as if unconsciously; by the reserved, fastidious hand of an artist, not by the gaudy fingers of a showman or the mechanical industry of a department-store window-dresser. As I remember it, in the twilight melancholy of that book, in its consistent mood, one can scarcely ever see the actual surroundings of the people; one feels them, rather, in the dusk.

Whatever is felt upon the page without being specifically named there — that, one might say, is created. It is the inexplicable presence of the thing not named, of the overtone divined by the ear but not heard by it, the verbal mood, the emotional aura of the fact or the thing or the deed, that gives high quality to the novel or the drama, as well as to poetry itself.

Literalness, when applied to the presenting of mental reactions and of physical sensations, seems to be no more effective than when it is applied to material things. A novel crowded with physical sensations is no less a catalogue than one crowded with furniture. A book like *The Rainbow* by D. H. Lawrence sharply reminds one how vast a distance lies between emotion and mere sensory reactions. Characters can be almost dehumanized by a laboratory study of the behaviour of their bodily organs under sensory stimuli — can be reduced, indeed, to mere animal pulp. Can one imagine anything more terrible than the story of *Romeo and Juliet* rewritten in prose by D. H. Lawrence?

How wonderful it would be if we could throw all the furniture out of the window; and along with it, all the meaningless reiterations concerning physical sensations, all the tiresome old patterns, and leave the room as bare as the stage of a Greek theatre, or as that house into which the glory of Pentecost descended; leave the scene bare for the play of emotions, great and little — for the nursery tale, no less than the tragedy, is killed by tasteless amplitude. The elder Dumas enunciated a great principle when he said that to make a drama, a man needed one passion, and four walls.

148 CHARLES STREET

Late in the winter of 1908 Mrs. Louis Brandeis conducted me along a noisy street in Boston and rang at a door hitherto unknown to me. Sometimes entering a new door can make a great change in one's life. That afternoon I had set out from the Parker House (the old, the real Parker House, before it was "modernized") to make a call on Mrs. Brandeis. When I reached her house in Otis Place she told me that we would go farther: she thought I would enjoy meeting a very charming old lady who was a near neighbour of hers, the widow of James T. Fields, of the publishing firm of Ticknor and Fields. The name of that firm meant something to me. In my father's bookcase there were little volumes of Longfellow and Hawthorne with that imprint. I wondered how the widow of one of the partners could still be living. Mrs. Brandeis explained that when James T. Fields was a man in middle life, a publisher of international reputation and a widower, he married Annie Adams, then a girl of nineteen. She had naturally survived him by many years.

When the door at 148 Charles Street was opened we waited a few moments in a small reception-room just off the hall, then went up a steep, thickly carpeted stairway and entered the "long drawing-room," where Mrs. Fields and Miss Jewett sat at tea. That room ran the depth of the house, its front windows, heavily curtained, on Charles Street, its back windows looking down on a deep garden. Directly above the garden wall lay the Charles River and, beyond, the Cambridge shore. At five o'clock in the afternoon the river was silvery from a half-hidden sun; over the great open space of water the western sky was dove-coloured with little ripples of rose. The air was full of soft moisture and the hint of approaching spring. Against this screen of pale winter light were the two ladies: Mrs. Fields reclining on a green sofa, directly under the youthful portrait of Charles Dickens (now in the Boston Art Museum), Miss Jewett seated, the low tea-table between them.

Mrs. Fields wore the widow's lavender which she never abandoned except for black velvet, with a scarf of Venetian lace on her hair. She was very slight and fragile in figure, with a great play of animation in her face and a delicate flush of pink on her cheeks. Like her friend Mrs. John Gardner, she had a skin which defied age. As for Miss Jewett — she looked very like the youthful picture of herself in the game of " Authors " I had played as a child, except that she was fuller in figure and a little grey. I do not at all remember what we talked about. Mrs.

Brandeis asked that I be shown some of the treasures of the house, but I had no eyes for the treasures, I was too intent upon the ladies.

That winter afternoon began a friendship, impoverished by Miss Jewett's death sixteen months later, but enduring until Mrs. Fields herself died, in February 1915.

In 1922 M. A. De Wolfe Howe, Mrs. Fields' literary executor, published a book of extracts from her diaries under the title *Memories of a Hostess*, a book which delighted all who had known her and many who had not, because of its vivid pictures of the Cambridge and Concord groups in the '60s and '70s, not as " celebrities " but as friends and fellow citizens. When Mr. Howe's book appeared, I wrote for *The Literary Review* an appreciation of it, very sketchy, but done with genuine enthusiasm, which I here incorporate without quotation marks.

In his book made up from the diaries of Mrs. James T. Fields, Mr. De Wolfe Howe presents a record of beautiful memories and, as its subtitle declares, " a chronicle of eminent friendships." For a period of sixty years Mrs. Fields' Boston house, at 148 Charles Street, extended its hospitality to the aristocracy of letters and art. During that long stretch of time there was scarcely an American of distinction in art or public life who was not a guest in that house; scarcely a visiting foreigner of renown who did not pay his tribute there.

It was not only men of letters, Dickens, Thackeray, and Matthew Arnold, who met Mrs. Fields' friends there; Salvini and Modjeska and Edwin Booth and Christine Nilsson and Joseph Jefferson and Ole Bull, Winslow Homer and Sargent, came and went, against the background of closely united friends who were a part of the very Charles Street scene. Longfellow, Emerson, Whittier, Hawthorne, Lowell, Sumner, Norton, Oliver Wendell Holmes — the list sounds like something in a school-book; but in Mrs. Fields' house one came to believe that they had been very living people — to feel that they had not been long absent from the rooms so full of their thoughts, of their letters, their talk, their remembrances sent at Christmas to the hostess, or brought to her from foreign lands. Even in the garden flourished guelder roses and flowering shrubs which some of these bearers of school-book names had brought in from Cambridge or Concord and set out there. At 148 Charles Street an American of the Apache period and territory could come to inherit a Colonial past.

Although Mrs. Fields was past seventy when I was first conducted into the long drawing-room, she did not seem old to me. Frail, diminished in force, yes; but, emphatically, *not* old. " The personal beauty of her younger years, long retained, and even at the end of such a stretch of life not quite lost," to quote Henry James, may have had something to do with the impression she gave; but I think it was even more because, as he also said of her, " all her implications were gay." I had seldom heard so young, so merry, so musical a laugh; a laugh with countless shades of relish and appreciation and kindness in it. And, on occasion, a short laugh from that same fragile source could positively do police duty! It could put an end to a conversation that had taken an unfortunate turn, absolutely dismiss and silence impertinence or presumption. No woman could have been so great a hostess, could have made so many highly developed personalities happy under her roof, could have blended so many strongly specialized and keenly sensitive people in her drawing-room, without having a great power to control and organize. It was a power so sufficient that one seldom felt it as one lived in the harmonious atmosphere it created — an atmosphere in which one seemed absolutely safe from everything ugly. Nobody can cherish the flower of social intercourse, can give it sun and sustenance and a tempered clime, without also being able very completely to dispose of anything that threatens it — not only the slug, but even the cold draught that ruffles its petals.

Mrs. Fields was in her own person flower-like; the remarkable fineness of her skin and pinkness of her cheeks gave one the comparison — and the natural ruby of her lips she never lost. It always struck one afresh (along with her clear eyes and their quick flashes of humour), that large, generous, mobile mouth, with its rich freshness of colour. " A *woman's* mouth," I used to think as I watched her talking to someone who pleased her; "not an old woman's! " One rejoiced in her little triumphs over colour-destroying age and its infirmities, as at the play one rejoices in the escape of the beautiful and frail from the pursuit of things powerful and evil. It was a drama in which the heroine must be sacrificed in the end: but for how long did she make the outward voyage delightful, with how many a *divertissement* and bright scene did she illumine the respite and the long wait at Aulis!

Sixty years of hospitality, so smooth and un-ruffled for the recipients, cost the hostess some-thing — cost her a great deal. The Fieldses were never people of liberal means, and the Charles Street house was not a convenient house to entertain in. The basement kitchen was a difficulty. On the first floor were the reception-room and the dining-room, on the second floor was the " long drawing-room," running the depth of the house. Mrs. Fields' own apartments were on the third floor, and the guest-rooms on the fourth. A house so constructed took a great deal of managing. Yet there was never an hour in the day when the order and calm of the drawing-room were not such that one might have sat down to write a sonnet or a sonata. The sweeping and dusting were done very early in the morning, the flowers arranged before the guests were awake.

Besides being distinctly young on the one hand, on the other Mrs. Fields seemed to me to reach back to Waterloo. As Mr. Howe reminds us, she had talked to Leigh Hunt about Shelley and his starlike beauty of face — and it is now more than a century since Shelley was drowned. She had known Severn well, and it was he who gave her a lock of Keats' hair, which, under glass with a drawing of Keats by the same artist, was one of the innumerable treasures of

that house. With so much to tell, Mrs. Fields
never became a set story-teller. She had no favourite stories — there were too many. Stories
were told from time to time, but only as things
of today reminded her of things of yesterday.
When we came home from the opera, she could
tell one what Chorley had said on such and such
an occasion. And then if one did not " go at "
her, but talked of Chorley just as if he were
Philip Hale or W. J. Henderson, one might
hear a great deal about him.

When one was staying at that house the past
lay in wait for one in all the corners; it exuded
from the furniture, from the pictures, the rare
editions, and the cabinets of manuscript — the
beautiful, clear manuscripts of a typewriterless
age, which even the printers had respected and
kept clean. The unique charm of Mrs. Fields'
house was not that it was a place where one
could hear about the past, but that it was a place
where the past lived on — where it was pro-
tected and cherished, had sanctuary from the
noisy push of the present. In casual conversa-

tion, at breakfast or tea, you might at any time unconsciously press a spring which liberated recollection, and one of the great shades seemed quietly to enter the room and to take the chair or the corner he had preferred in life.

One afternoon I showed her an interesting picture of Pauline Viardot I had brought from Paris, and my hostess gave me such an account of hearing Viardot sing Gluck's *Orpheus* that I felt I had heard it myself. Then she told me how, when she saw Dickens in London, just after he had returned from giving a reading in Paris, he said: " Oh, yes, the house was sold out. But the important thing is that Viardot came, and sat in a front seat and never took her glorious eyes off me. So, of course," with a flourish of his hand, " nothing else mattered! " A little-known Russian gentleman, Mr. Turgeniev, must have been staying at Madame Viardot's country house at that time. Did he accompany her to the reading, one wonders? If he had, it would probably have meant very little to " Mr. Dickens."

It was at tea-time, I used to think, that the

great shades were most likely to appear; sometimes they seemed to come up the deeply carpeted stairs, along with living friends. At that hour the long room was dimly lighted, the fire bright, and through the wide windows the sunset was flaming, or softly brooding, upon the Charles River and the Cambridge shore beyond. The ugliness of the world, all possibility of wrenches and jars and wounding contacts, seemed securely shut out. It was indeed the peace of the past, where the tawdry and cheap have been eliminated and the enduring things have taken their proper, happy places.

Mrs. Fields read aloud beautifully, especially Shakespeare and Milton, for whom she had, even in age, a wonderful depth of voice. I loved to hear her read *Richard II*, or the great, melancholy speeches of *Henry IV* in the Palace at Westminster:

> " And changes fill the cup of altera-ti-on
> With divers liquors."

Many of those lines I can only remember with

the colour, the slight unsteadiness, of that fine
old voice.

Once I was sitting on the sofa beside her,
helping her to hold a very heavy, very old, calf-
bound Milton, while she read:

" In courts and palaces he also reigns,
  And in luxurious cities, where the noise
  Of riot ascends above their loftiest towers,
  And injury and outrage."

When she paused in the solemn evocation for
breath, I tried to fill in the interval by saying
something about such lines calling up the tumult
of Rome and Babylon.

" Or New York," she said slyly, glancing side-
wise, and then at once again attacked the mighty
page.

Naturally, she was rich in reference and quotation. I recall how she once looked up from a
long reverie and said: " You know, my dear, I
think we sometimes forget how much we owe
to Dryden's prefaces." To my shame, I have not
to this day discovered the full extent of my in-

debtedness. On another occasion Mrs. Fields murmured something about " A *bracelet of bright hair about the bone.*" " That's very nice," said I, " but I don't recognize it."

" Surely," she said, " that would be Dr. Donne."

I never pretended to Mrs. Fields — I would have had to pretend too much. " And who," I brazenly asked, " was Dr. Donne? "

I knew before morning. She had a beautiful patience with Bœotian ignorance, but I was strongly encouraged to take two fat volumes of Dr. Donne to bed with me that night.

I love to remember one charming visit in her summer house at Manchester-by-the-Sea, when Sarah Orne Jewett was there. I had just come from Italy bringing word of the places they most loved and about which they had often written me, entreating, nay, commanding me to visit them. Had I gone riding on the Pincian Hill? Mrs. Fields asked. No, I hadn't; I didn't think many people rode there now. Well, said Mrs. Fields, the Brownings' little boy used to ride there, in his velvets. When he complained to her that the Pincio was the same every day, no variety, she suggested that he might ride out into the Campagna. But he sighed and shook his head. " Oh, no! My pony and I have to go there. We are one of the sights of Rome, you know! " As this was the son of a friend, one didn't comment upon the child's speech or the future it suggested.

The second evening after my arrival happened to be a rainy one — no visitors. After dinner Mrs. Fields began to read a little — warmed to her work, and read all of Matthew Arnold's *Scholar Gypsy* and *Tristan and Iseult*. Miss Jewett said she didn't believe the latter poem had been read aloud in that house since Matthew Arnold himself read it there.

At Manchester, when there were no guests, Mrs. Fields had tea on the back veranda, overlooking a wild stretch of woodland. Down in this wood, directly beneath us, were a tea-table and seats built under the trees, where they used to have tea when the hostess was younger — now the climb was too steep for her. It was a little sad, perhaps, to sit and look out over a shrinking kingdom; but if she felt it, she never showed it. Miss Jewett and I went down into the wood, and she told me she hated to go there now, as it reminded her that much was already lost, and what was left was so at the mercy of chance! It seemed as if a strong wind might blow away that beloved friend of many years. We talked in low voices. Who could have believed that Mrs. Fields was to outlive Miss Jewett, so much the younger, by nearly six years, as she outlived Mr. Fields by thirty-four! She had the very genius of survival. She was not, as she once laughingly told me, " to escape anything, not even free verse or the Cubists! " She was not in the least dashed by either. Oh, no, she said, the Cubists weren't any queerer than Manet and the Impressionists were when they first came to Boston, and people used to run in for tea and ask her whether she had ever heard of such a thing as " blue snow," or a man's black hat being purple in the sun!

As in Boston tea was the most happy time for reminiscences, in Manchester it was at the breakfast hour that they were most likely to throng. Breakfasts were long, as country breakfasts have a right to be. We had always been out of doors first and were very hungry.

One morning when the cantaloupes were particularly fine Mrs. Fields began to tell me of Henry James' father, — apropos of the melons, though I forget whether it was that he liked them very much or couldn't abide them. She told me a great deal about him; but I was most interested in what she said regarding his faith in his son. When the young man's first essays and stories began to come back across the Atlantic from Rome and Paris they did not meet with approval in Boston; they were thought self-conscious, artificial, shallow. His father's friends feared the young man had mistaken his calling. Mr. James the elder, however, was altogether pleased. He came down to Manchester one summer to have a talk with the great publisher about Henry, and expressed his satisfaction and confidence. " Believe me," he said, sitting at this very table, " the boy will make his mark in letters, Fields."

The next summer I was visiting Mrs. Fields at Manchester in a season of intense heat. We were daily expecting the arrival of Henry James, Jr., himself. One morning came a spluttery letter from the awaited friend, containing bitter references to the " Great American summer," and saying that he was " lying at Nahant," prostrated by the weather. I was very much disappointed, but Mrs. Fields said wisely: " My dear, it is just as well. Mr. James is always greatly put about by the heat, and at Nahant there is the chance of a breeze."

The house at Manchester was called Thunderbolt Hill. Mr. Howe thinks the name incongruous, but that depends on what associations you choose to give it. When I went a-calling with Mrs. Fields and left her card with Thunderbolt Hill engraved in the corner, I felt that I was paying calls with the lady Juno herself. Why shouldn't such a name befit a hill of high decisions and judgments? Moreover, Mrs. Fields was not at all responsible for that name; it came, as she and Miss Jewett liked proverbs and place-names to come, from the native folk. Long years before James T. Fields bought the hill to build a summer cottage, some fine trees at the top of it had been destroyed by lightning; the country people thereabouts had ever afterward called it Thunderbolt Hill.

Mrs. Fields' Journal tells us how in her young married days she always moved from Boston to Manchester-by-the-Sea in early summer, just as she still did when I knew her. I remember one characteristic passage in the Journal, written at Manchester and dated July 16, 1870:

It is a perfect summer day, she says. Mr. Fields does not go up to town but stays at home with a bag full of MSS. He and his wife go to a favourite spot in a pasture by the sea, and she reads him a new story which has just come in from Henry James, Jr., then a very young man — *Compagnons de Voyage*, in " execrable " handwriting. They find the quality good. " I do not know," Mrs. Fields wrote in her diary that evening, " why success in work should affect one so powerfully, but I could have wept as I finished reading, not from the sweet, low pathos of the tale, but from the knowledge of the writer's success. It is so difficult to do anything well in this mysterious world."

Yes, one says to oneself, that is Mrs. Fields, at her best. She rose to meet a fine performance, always — to the end. At eighty she could still entertain new people, new ideas, new forms of art. And she brought to her greeting of the new all the richness of her rich past: a long, unbroken chain of splendid contacts, beautiful friendships.

As one follows the diary down through the years, the reader must feel a certain pride in the determined way in which the New England group refused to be patronized by glittering foreign celebrities — by any celebrities! At dinner Dr. Holmes holds himself a little apart from the actor guests, Jefferson and Warren, and addresses them as " you gentlemen of the stage " in a way that quite disturbed Longfellow and, one may judge, the hostess. They all come to dine with Dickens in his long stays with the Fieldses, come repeatedly, but they seem ever a little on their guard. Emerson cannot be got to believe him altogether genuine and sincere. He insists to Mrs. Fields that Dickens has " too much talent for his genius," and that he is " too consummate an artist to have a thread of nature left "! Thackeray made a long visit at 148 Charles Street. (It is said that he finished *Henry Esmond* there.) In the guest-room which he occupied, with an alcove study, hung a little drawing he had made of himself, framed with the note he had written the hostess telling her that, happy as he was here, he must go home to England for Christmas.

When Mrs. Fields was still a young woman, she noted in her diary that Aristotle says: " Virtue is concerned with action; art with production." " The problem in life," she adds, " is to harmonize these two." In a long life she went far toward working out this problem. She knew how to appreciate the noble in behaviour and the noble in art. In the patriot, the philanthropist, the statesman, she could forgive abominable taste. In the artist, the true artist, she could forgive vanity, sensitiveness, selfishness, indecision, and vacillation of will. She was generous and just in her judgment of men and women because she understood Aristotle's axiom. " With a great gift," I once heard her murmur thoughtfully, " we must be willing to bear greatly, because it has already greatly borne."

Today, in 1936, a garage stands on the site of 148 Charles Street. Only in memory exists the long, green-carpeted, softly lighted drawing-room, and the dining-table where Learning and Talent met, enjoying good food and good wit and rare vintages, looking confidently forward to the growth of their country in the finer amenities of life. Perhaps the garage and all it stands for represent the only real development, and have altogether taken the place of things formerly cherished on that spot. If we try to imagine those dinner-parties which Mrs. Fields describes, the scene is certainly not to us what it was to her: the lighting has changed, and the guests seem hundreds of years away from us. Their portraits no longer hang on the walls of our academies, nor are their " works " much discussed there. The English classes, we are told, can be " interested " only in contemporary writers, the newer the better. A letter from a prep-school boy puts it tersely: " D. H. Lawrence is rather rated a back-number here, but Faulkner keeps his end up."

Not the prep-school boys only are blithe to leave the past untroubled: their instructors pretty generally agree with them. And the retired professors who taught these instructors do not see Shelley plain as they once did. The faith of the elders has been shaken.

Just how did this change come about, one wonders. When and where were the Arnolds overthrown and the Brownings devaluated? Was it at the Marne? At Versailles, when a new geography was being made on paper? Certainly the literary world which emerged from the war used a new coinage. In England and America the " masters " of the last century diminished in stature and pertinence, became remote and shadowy.

But Mrs. Fields never entered this strange

twilight. She rounded out her period, from Dickens and Thackeray and Tennyson, through Hardy and Meredith to the Great War, with her standards unshaken. For her there was no revaluation. She died with her world (the world of " letters " which mattered most to her) unchallenged. Marcel Proust somewhere said that when he came to die he would take all his great men with him: since his Beethoven and his Wagner could never be at all the same to anyone else, they would go with him like the captives who were slain at the funeral pyres of Eastern potentates. It was thus Mrs. Fields died, in that house of memories, with the material keepsakes of the past about her.

MISS JEWETT[1]

I

In reading over a package of letters from Sarah Orne Jewett, I find this observation: *" The thing that teases the mind over and over for years, and at last gets itself put down rightly on paper — whether little or great, it belongs to Literature."* Miss Jewett was very conscious of the fact that when a writer makes anything that belongs to

[1] Much of Part I of this sketch was originally written as a preface to a two-volume collection of Miss Jewett's stories published by Houghton Mifflin in 1925.

Literature (limiting the term here to imaginative literature, which she of course meant), his material goes through a process very different from that by which he makes merely a good story. No one can define this process exactly; but certainly persistence, survival, recurrence in the writer's mind, are highly characteristic of it. The shapes and scenes that have " teased " the mind for years, when they do at last get themselves rightly put down, make a much higher order of writing, and a much more costly, than the most vivid and vigorous transfer of immediate impressions.

In some of Miss Jewett's earlier books, *Deephaven*, *Country Byways*, *Old Friends and New*, one can find first sketches, first impressions, which later crystallized into almost flawless examples of literary art. One can, as it were, watch in process the two kinds of making: the first, which is full of perception and feeling but rather fluid and formless; the second, which is tightly built and significant in design. The design is, indeed, so happy, so right, that it seems inevitable; the de-

sign is the story and the story is the design. The
" Pointed Fir " sketches are living things caught
in the open, with light and freedom and air-
spaces about them. They melt into the land and
the life of the land until they are not stories at all,
but life itself.

A great many stories were being written upon
New England themes at the same time that Miss
Jewett was writing; stories that to many contemporary readers may have seemed more interesting
than hers, because they dealt with more definite
" situations " and were more heavily accented.
But they are not very interesting to reread today;
they have not the one thing that survives all arresting situations, all good writing and clever story-
making — inherent, individual beauty.

Walter Pater said that every truly great drama
must, in the end, linger in the reader's mind as a
sort of ballad. One might say that every fine
story must leave in the mind of the sensitive
reader an intangible residuum of pleasure; a
cadence, a quality of voice that is exclusively

the writer's own, individual, unique. A quality which one can remember without the volume at hand, can experience over and over again in the mind but can never absolutely define, as one can experience in memory a melody, or the summer perfume of a garden. The magnitude of the subject-matter is not of primary importance, seemingly. An idyll of Theocritus, concerned with sheep and goats and shade and pastures, is today as much alive as the most dramatic passages of the *Iliad* — stirs the reader's feeling quite as much, perhaps.

It is a common fallacy that a writer, if he is talented enough, can achieve this poignant quality by improving upon his subject-matter, by using his " imagination " upon it and twisting it to suit his purpose. The truth is that by such a process (which is not imaginative at all!) he can at best produce only a brilliant sham, which, like a badly built and pretentious house, looks poor and shabby after a few years. If he achieves anything noble, anything enduring, it must be by giving himself absolutely to his material. And this gift of sympathy is his great gift; is the fine thing in him that alone can make his work fine.

The artist spends a lifetime in pursuing the things that haunt him, in having his mind " teased " by them, in trying to get these concep‑ tions down on paper exactly as they are to him and not in conventional poses supposed to reveal their character; trying this method and that, as a painter tries different lightings and different at‑ titudes with his subject to catch the one that presents it more suggestively than any other. And at the end of a lifetime he emerges with much that is more or less happy experimenting, and comparatively little that is the very flower of him‑ self and his genius.

The best of Miss Jewett's work, read by a stu‑ dent fifty years from now, will give him the char‑ acteristic flavour, the spirit, the cadence, of an American writer of the first order, — and of a New England which will then be a thing of the past.

Even in the stories which fall short of being Miss Jewett's best, one has the pleasure of her society and companionship — if one likes that sort of companionship. I remember she herself had a fondness for " The Hiltons' Holiday," — the slightest of stories: a hard-worked New England farmer takes his two little girls to town, some seventeen miles away (a long drive by wagon), for a treat. That is all, yet the story is a little miracle. It simply *is the look* — shy, kind, a little wistful — which shines out at one from good country faces on remote farms; it is the look *itself.* To have got it down upon the printed page is like bringing the tenderest of early spring flowers from the deep wood into the hot light of noon without bruising its petals.

To note an artist's limitations is but to define his talent. A reporter can write equally well about everything that is presented to his view, but a creative writer can do his best only with what lies within the range and character of his deepest sympathies. These stories of Miss Jewett's have much to do with fisher-folk and seaside villages; with juniper pastures and lonely farms, neat grey country houses and delightful, well-seasoned old

men and women. That, when one thinks of it
in a flash, is New England. I remember hearing an
English actor say that until he made a motor trip
through the New England country he had supposed that the Americans killed their aged in some
merciful fashion, for he saw none in the cities
where he played.

There are many kinds of people in the State of
Maine, and neighbouring States, who are not
found in Miss Jewett's books. There may be
Othellos and Iagos and Don Juans; but they are
not highly characteristic of the country, they do
not come up spontaneously in the juniper pastures as the everlasting does. Miss Jewett wrote of
everyday people who grew out of the soil, not
about exceptional individuals at war with their
environment. This was not a creed with her, but
an instinctive preference.

Born within the scent of the sea but not within
sight of it, in a beautiful old house full of strange
and lovely things brought home from all over the
globe by seafaring ancestors, she spent much of
her childhood driving about the country with her

doctor father on his professional rounds among the farms. She early learned to love her country for what it was. What is quite as important, she saw it as it was. She happened to have the right nature, the right temperament, to see it so — and to understand by intuition the deeper meaning of what she saw.

She had not only the eye, she had the ear. From her early years she must have treasured up those pithy bits of local speech, of native idiom, which enrich and enliven her pages. The language her people speak to each other is a native tongue. No writer can invent it. It is made in the hard school of experience, in communities where language has been undisturbed long enough to take on colour and character from the nature and experiences of the people. The " sayings " of a community, its proverbs, are its characteristic comment upon life; they imply its history, suggest its attitude toward the world and its way of accepting life. Such an idiom makes the finest language any writer can have; and he can never get it with a notebook. He himself must be able to think and feel in that speech — it is a gift from heart to heart.

Much of Miss Jewett's delightful humour comes from her delicate and tactful handling of this native language of the waterside and countryside, never overdone, never pushed a shade too far; from this, and from her own fine attitude toward her subject-matter. This attitude in itself, though unspoken, is everywhere felt, and constitutes one of the most potent elements of grace and charm in her stories. She had with her own stories and her own characters a very charming relation; spirited, gay, tactful, noble in its essence and a little arch in its expression. In this particular relationship many of our most gifted writers are unfortunate. If a writer's attitude toward his characters and his scene is as vulgar as a showman's, as mercenary as an auctioneer's, vulgar and meretricious will his product for ever remain.

II

" The distinguished outward stamp " — it was that one felt immediately upon meeting Miss

Jewett: a lady, in the old high sense. It was in her face and figure, in her carriage, her smile, her voice, her way of greeting one. There was an ease, a graciousness, a light touch in conversation, a delicate unobtrusive wit. You quickly recognized that her gift with the pen was one of many charming personal attributes. In the short period when I knew her, 1908 and 1909, she was not writing at all, and found life full enough without it. Some six years before, she had been thrown from a carriage on a country road (sad fate for an enthusiastic horsewoman) and suffered a slight concussion. She recovered, after a long illness, but she did not write again — felt that her best working power was spent.

She had never been one of those who " live to write." She lived for a great many things, and the stories by which we know her were one of many preoccupations. After the carriage accident she was not strong enough to go out into the world a great deal; before that occurred her friendships occupied perhaps the first place in her life. She had friends among the most interesting and gifted people of her time, and scores of friends among the village and country people of her own State — people who knew her as Doctor Jewett's daughter and regarded " Sarah's writing " as a ladylike accomplishment. These country friends, she used to say, were the wisest of all, because they could never be fooled about fundamentals. Even after her long illness she was at home to a few visitors almost every afternoon; friends from England and France were always coming and going. Small dinner-parties and luncheons were part of the regular routine when she was with Mrs. Fields on Charles Street or at Manchester-by-the-Sea. When she was at home, in South Berwick, there were the old friends of her childhood to whom she must be always accessible. At the time I knew her she had, as she said, forgone all customary exercises — except a little gardening in spring and summer. But as a young woman she devoted her mornings to horseback riding in fine weather, and was skilful with a sailboat. Every day, in every season of the year, she enjoyed the beautiful country in which she had the good fortune to be born. Her love of the Maine country and seacoast was the supreme happiness of her life. Her stories were but reflections, quite incidental, of that peculiar and intensely personal pleasure. Take, for instance, that clear, daybreak paragraph which begins " By the Morning Boat ":

" On the coast of Maine, where many green islands and salt inlets fringe the deep-cut shore line; where balsam firs and bayberry bushes send their fragrance far seaward, and song-sparrows sing all day, and the tide runs plashing in and out among the weedy ledges; where cowbells tinkle on the hills and herons stand in the shady coves — on the lonely coast of Maine stood a small gray house facing the morning light."

Wherever Miss Jewett might be in the world, in the Alps, the Pyrenees, the Apennines, she carried the Maine shore-country with her. She loved it by instinct, and in the light of wide experience, from near and from afar.

" You must know the world before you can know the village," she once said to me. Quoted out of its context this remark sounds like a wise pronouncement, but Miss Jewett never made wise pronouncements. Her personal opinions she voiced lightly, half-humorously; any expression of them was spontaneous, the outgrowth of the immediate conversation. This remark was a supplementary comment, apropos of a story we had both happened to read: a story about a mule, introduced by the magazine which published it with an editorial note to the effect that (besides being " fresh " and " promising ") it was authentic, as the young man who wrote it was a mule-driver and had never been anything else. When I asked Miss Jewett if she had seen it, she gave no affirmative but a soft laugh, rather characteristic of her, something between amusement and forbearance, and exclaimed:

" Poor lad! But his mule could have done better! A mule, by God's grace, is a mule, with the mettle of his kind. Besides, the mule would be grammatical. It's not in his sure-footed nature to slight syntax. A horse might tangle himself up in his sentences or his picket rope, but never a mule."

III

Miss Jewett had read too widely, and had too fine a literary sense, to overestimate her own performance. Every Sunday book section of the New York dailies announces half a dozen "great" books, and calls our attention to more great writers than the Elizabethan age and the nineteenth century put together could muster. Miss Jewett applied that adjective very seldom (to Tolstoi, Flaubert, and a few others), certainly never to herself or to anything of her own. She spoke of "the Pointed Fir papers" or "the Pointed Fir sketches"; I never heard her call them stories. She had, as Henry James said of her, "a sort of elegance of humility, or fine flame of modesty." She was content to be slight, if she could be true. The closing sentences of "Marsh Rosemary" might stand as an unconscious piece of self-criticism, — or perhaps as a gentle apology for the art of all new countries, which must grow out of a thin soil and bear its fate:

" Who can laugh at my Marsh Rosemary, or who can cry, for that matter? The gray primness of the plant is made up from a hundred colors if you look close enough to find them. This Marsh Rosemary stands in her own place, and holds her dry leaves and tiny blossoms steadily toward the same sun that the pink lotus blooms for, and the white rose."

For contemporary writers of much greater range than her own, she had the most reverent and rejoicing admiration. She was one of the first Americans to see the importance of Joseph Conrad. Indeed, she was reading a new volume of Conrad, late in the night, when the slight cerebral hæmorrhage occurred from which she died some months later.

At a time when machine-made historical novels were the literary fashion in the United States, when the magazines were full of dreary dialect stories, and the works of John Fox, Jr., were considered profound merely because they were very dull and heavy as clay, Miss Jewett quietly developed her own medium and confined herself to it. At that time Henry James was the commanding figure in American letters, and his was surely the keenest mind any American ever devoted to the art of fiction. But it was devoted almost exclusively to the study of other and older societies than ours. He was interested in his countrymen chiefly as they appeared in relation to the European scene. As an American writer he seems to claim, and richly to deserve, a sort of personal exemption. Stephen Crane came upon the scene, a young man of definite talent, brilliant and brittle, — dealing altogether with the surfaces of things, but in a manner all his own. He died young, but he had done something real. One can read him today. If we glance back over the many novels which have challenged our attention since Crane's time, it is like taking a stroll through a World's Fair grounds some years after the show is over. Palaces with the stucco peeling off, oriental villages stripped to beaver-board and cement, broken fountains, lakes gone to mud and weeds. We realize that whatever it is that makes a book hold together, most of these hadn't it.

Among those glittering novelties which have now become old-fashioned Miss Jewett's little volumes made a small showing. A taste for them must always remain a special taste, — but it will remain. She wrote for a limited audience, and she still has it, both here and abroad. To enjoy her the reader must have a sympathetic relation with the subject-matter and a sensitive ear; especially must he have a sense of " pitch " in writing. He must recognize when the quality of feeling comes inevitably out of the theme itself; when the language, the stresses, the very structure of the sentences are imposed upon the writer by the special mood of the piece.

It is easy to understand why some of the young students who have turned back from the present to glance at Miss Jewett find very little on her pages. Imagine a young man, or woman, born in

Miss Jewett

New York City, educated at a New York university, violently inoculated with Freud, hurried into journalism, knowing no more about New England country people (or country folk anywhere) than he has caught from motor trips or observed from summer hotels: what is there for him in *The Country of the Pointed Firs?*

This hypothetical young man is perhaps of foreign descent: German, Jewish, Scandinavian. To him English is merely a means of making himself understood, of communicating his ideas. He may write and speak American English correctly, but only as an American may learn to speak French correctly. It is a surface speech: he clicks the words out as a bank clerk clicks out silver when you ask for change. For him the language has no emotional roots. How could he find the talk of the Maine country people anything but " dialect "? Moreover, the temper of the people which lies behind the language is incomprehensible to him. He can see what these Yankees *have not* (hence an epidemic of " suppressed desire " plays and novels), but what they *have*, their actual preferences and their fixed scale of values, are absolutely dark to him. When he tries to put himself in the Yankee's place, he attempts an impossible substitution.

But the adopted American is not alone in being cut off from an instinctive understanding of " the old moral harmonies." There is the new American, whom Mr. Santayana describes as " the untrained, pushing, cosmopolitan orphan, cocksure in manner but none too sure in his morality, to whom the old Yankee, with his sour integrity, is almost a foreigner." [1]

When we find ourselves on shipboard, among hundreds of strangers, we very soon recognize those who are sympathetic to us. We find our own books in the same way. We like a writer much as we like individuals; for what he is, simply, underneath his accomplishments. Oftener than we realize, it is for some moral quality, some ideal which he himself cherishes, though it may be little

[1] George Santayana: *Character and Opinion in the United States.* New York: Charles Scribner's Sons; 1920.

discernible in his behaviour in the world. It is the light behind his books and is the living quality in his sentences.

It is this very personal quality of perception, a vivid and intensely personal experience of life, which make a " style "; Mark Twain had it, at his best, and Hawthorne. But among fifty thousand books you will find very few writers who ever achieved a style at all. The distinctive thing about Miss Jewett is that she had an individual voice; " a sense for the finest kind of truthful rendering, the sober, tender note, the temperately touched, whether in the ironic or pathetic," as Henry James said of her. During the twenty-odd clamorous years since her death " masterpieces " have been bumping down upon us like trunks pouring down the baggage chutes from an overcrowded ocean steamer. But if you can get out from under them and go to a quiet spot and take up a volume of Miss Jewett, you will find the voice still there, with a quality which any ear trained in literature must recognize.

"JOSEPH AND HIS BROTHERS"

I

In the Prologue of his great work Thomas
Mann says of it: " Its theme is the first and last of
all our questioning and speaking and all our necessity; the nature of man." But it is not the nature of man as the Behaviourists or the biologists
see it. This is a double nature, struggling with
itself, and the struggle is not to keep the physical
machine running smoothly. These ancient people
know very little about their physical structure.
Their attention is fixed upon something within

themselves which they feel to be their real life, consciousness; where it came from and what becomes of it. In this book men ask themselves the questions they asked æons ago when they found themselves in an unconscious world. From the Old Testament, that greatest record of the orphan soul trying to find its kin somewhere in the universe, and from the cruder superstitions of the neighbouring Semitic peoples, Mann has made something like an orchestral arrangement of all the Semitic religions and philosophies.

There are two ways in which a story-teller can approach a theme set in the distant past. The way most familiar to us is that which Flaubert took in *Salammbô*. The writer stands in present time, his own time, and looks backward. He works and thinks in a long-vanished society. His mind is naturally fixed upon contrasting that world with our own; upon religions, institutions, manners, ways of thinking, all very unlike ours. The reader sees the horrors and splendours of *Salammbô* from a distance; partly because it was a point of ethics with Flaubert to encourage no familiarity at any time, but particularly because in this book he himself was engaged with the feeling of distance, strangeness, difference.

Mann approaches an even more distant past by another route; he gets behind the epoch of his story and looks forward. He begins with a Prologue which is informed by all the discoveries science has lately made about the beginnings of human existence on this globe; the beginnings long before the known beginning, the long ages when men "did battle with the flying newts" and life was little more than a misery which persisted. From the depths without a history he comes up through the ages of orally transmitted legend; every legend, he believes, having a fact behind it, an occurrence of critical importance to the breed of man.

After the tremendous preparation of the Prologue (a marvel of imaginative power), he rises out of the bottomless depths to the period of his story; not much more than three thousand years ago, he says, when men were very much like ourselves, "aside from a measure of dreamy indefiniteness in their habits of thought."

This same dreamy indefiniteness, belonging to a people without any of the relentless mechanical gear which directs every moment of modern life toward accuracy, this indefiniteness is one of the most effective elements of verity in this great work. We are among a shepherd people; the story has almost the movement of grazing sheep. The characters live at that pace. Perhaps no one who has not lived among sheep can realize the rightness of the rhythm. A shepherd people is not driving toward anything. With them, truly, as Michelet said of quite another form of journeying, the end is nothing, the road is all. In fact, the road and the end are literally one.

There is nothing in *Joseph and His Brothers* more admirable than the tempo, the deliberate, sustained pace. (In this age of blinding speed and shattering sound!) Never was there a happier conjunction of writer and subject-matter. Thomas Mann's natural tempo is deliberate; his sentences come out of reflection, not out of an impulse. It is possible for him to write the story of a shepherd people at the right pace and with the right kind of development, — continual circling and digression — which here is not digression since it is his purpose. He can listen to the herdsmen telling their stories over and over, go backward and forward with their " dreamily indefinite " habits of thought. He has all the time there is; Mediterranean time, 1700 B.C.

When I refer to a passage in the book to refresh my memory, I find myself reading on and on, largely from pleasure in this rich deliberateness which is never without intensity and deep vibration. It is not a kind of writing adapted to all subjects, certainly, but here it is in the very nature of the theme; it gives, along with this distinctive rhythm, a warm homeliness, communicates a brooding tenderness which is in the author's mind. For in this book Herr Mann is enamoured of his theme, wholly given to it, and this favouritism, held in check by his native temperateness, is itself a source of pleasure; the strong feeling under the strong hand.

"*Joseph and His Brothers*"

At the end of his Prologue the author declares that he is glad to come up from the bottomless pit of prehistoric struggle, and the undecipherable riddle of the old legends, to something relatively near, rather like a home-coming. We, too, are glad. With a sense of escape we approach something already known to us; not glacier ages or a submerged Atlantis, but the very human Mediterranean shore, on a moonlight night in the season of spring.

We have all been there before, even if we have never crossed salt water. (Perhaps this is not strictly accurate, but even the Agnostic and the Behaviourist would have to admit that his great-grandfather had been there.) The Bible countries along the Mediterranean shore were very familiar to most of us in our childhood. Whether we were born in New Hampshire or Virginia or California, Palestine lay behind us. We took it in unconsciously and unthinkingly perhaps, but we could not escape it. It was all about us, in the pictures on the walls, in the songs we sang in Sunday school, in the " opening exercises " at day school, in the talk of the old people, wherever we lived. And it was in our language — fixedly, indelibly. The effect of the King James translation of the Bible upon English prose has been repeated down through the generations, leaving its mark on the minds of all children who had any but the most sluggish emotional nature.

We emerge from Mann's Prologue to find ourselves not only in a familiar land, but among people we have always known, Joseph and Jacob: and they are talking about their remote ancestors, whom we also know. The Book of Genesis lies like a faded tapestry deep in the consciousness of almost every individual who is more than forty years of age. Moreover, as it is the background of nearly all the art of Western Europe, even today's college Senior must have come upon it, if only by the cheerless road of reference reading. We are familiar with Mann's characters and their history, not only through Moses and the Prophets, but through Milton and Dante and Racine, Bach and Hayden and Handel, through painters and architects and stone-cutters innumerable. We

"Joseph and His Brothers"

begin the book with the great imaginings and the great imaginators already in our minds — we are dyed through and through with them. That is the take-off of the story.

II

The first volume of the work is the book of Jacob, — of Jacob and his forbears. In a family which held itself so much apart from other tribes and sects, the connection between each man and a long line of grandfathers was very close. There were external features common to all the Semitic religions; hence the shallow and light-minded of the descendants of Abraham were often backsliders, marrying with women of other tribes and troubling themselves very little about the one great idea that had brought Abraham out of Chaldea and isolated him from his own and all other peoples. Whenever that conception of God was very strong in one of Abraham's descendants (was indeed the burning purpose of his inner life, as it was of Jacob's), that man was virtually Abraham's grandson, no matter how many physical generations had gone between, and he was the true and direct inheritor of the " blessing," aside from any accident of primogeniture.

Throughout this first volume one gradually becomes aware that Abraham's seed were not so much the " chosen people " as they were *the people who chose.* They chose to renounce not only sacred images, " idols," but all the spells and incantations and rites to which men resorted for comfort of mind, and to wander forth searching for a God of whom no image could be made by mortal hand. A God who was not a form, but a force, an essence; felt, but not imprisoned in matter. " The God of the ages," Mann puts it, " for whom he [Abraham] sought a name and found none sufficient, wherefore he gave Him the plural, calling Him, provisionally, Elohim, the Godhead."

Herr Mann accounts for Abraham's quest in this wise:

" What had set him in motion was unrest of the spirit, a need of God, and if — as there can be no doubt — dispensations were vouchsafed him, they had reference to the irradiations of his personal experience of God, which was of a new kind altogether; and his whole concern from the beginning had been to win for it sympathy and adherence. He suffered; and when he compared the measure of his inward distress with that of the great majority, he drew the conclusion that it was pregnant with the future. Not in vain, so he heard from the newly beheld God, shall have been thy torment and thine unrest; for it shall fructify many souls and make proselytes in numbers like to the sands of the seas; and it shall give impulse to great expansions of life hidden in it as in a seed; and in one word, thou shalt be a blessing. A blessing? It is unlikely that the word gives the true meaning of that which happened to him in his very sight and which corresponded to his temperament and to his experience of himself. For the word ' blessing ' carries with it an idea which but ill describes men of his sort: men, that is, of roving spirit and discomfortable mind, whose novel conception of the deity is destined to make its mark upon the future. The life of men with whom new histories begin can seldom or never be a sheer unclouded blessing; not this it is which their consciousness of self whispers in their ears. ' And thou shalt be a destiny ': such is the purer and more precise meaning of the promise, in whatever language it may have been spoken."

The idea was a leap centuries ahead into the dark. Yet it must have been born in the mind of one man: such revelations never come to committees or bureaus of research. Abraham's descendants could not always live up to it, but tradition held them together, and the rite of circumcision set them apart. The rite and the form can be continued even in the sluggish generations when the significance is lost. But Mann's work begins when the quest which drove Abraham out of a stupefied materialistic world is burning bright again in Jacob, who, by stratagems outwardly crooked but inwardly inevitable, " had saved his life, his precious, covenanted life, for God and the future."

Jacob, apparently, was the first of Abraham's descendants who had the power of realizing and experiencing God more and more sharply through all the variations of a life incredibly eventful and long. He experienced Him in meditation, in the unforeseeable but strangely logical working-out of events in his own life — and in dreams. Dreams so full of meaning that they were to him promises. After Abraham's people had cut themselves off from the comfortableness and commonplaceness of anthropomorphic gods, there still remained the ladder of dreams, by which the orphan soul could mount and the ministers of grace descend.

Jacob the constant lover, who served seven years for Rachel: the trickery of Laban: the rivalry between the sisters: these are great stories which have lived through the centuries. But the greatest, the most moving story is what the author terms "Jacob's labouring upon the Godhead." Jacob is a many-sided man, — but the painting of his contradictions must be left to Thomas Mann himself. He has done it as no one else could. The creation of Jacob, in the flesh and in the spirit, is the great achievement of his work. The man who knows that he bears the " blessing " and who sees further into destiny than any of his tribe or time, must, sometimes by purposed indirection, sometimes by stepping aside and shutting his eyes, " save his precious, covenanted life for God and the future." For the aim of the law is worth more than any letter of it, and a trivial transaction or a question of family government must not be allowed to interfere with those fruitful seasons of thought which are well called " labour upon the Godhead."

For every lapse in conduct and shirking of responsibility Jacob paid, of course. But the payment, however cruel, seems always to set him a long way forward in his incommunicable spiritual quest, — which certainly proves that his way was for him the right way. With every sorrow he brought upon himself for failing in a plain duty, the immortal jewel he carried within became brighter, and his faith in the way his fathers had chosen more sure. His shirking in the matter of restraining Leah's sons from their revenge for Dinah cost him Rachel, who died because she was forced to travel by mule-back when she was close upon her confinement. (Another contributing cause comes in here, very characteristic of Jacob, and, one might say, of the author's mind as well.) Rachel died by the roadside, giving birth to Benjamin. It was as Jacob sat beside her under the mulberry tree, aware that she was dying, that there came over him the greatest of his understandings, loftier than all his visions:

" And then it was that he directed upwards into the silvery light of those worlds above their heads, almost as a confession that he understood, his question: 'Lord, what dost Thou?'

" To such questions there is no answer. Yet it is the glory of the human spirit that in this silence it does not depart from God, but rather learns to grasp the majesty of the ungraspable and to thrive thereon. Beside him the Chaldæan women and slaves chanted their litanies and

invocations, thinking to bind to human wishes
the unreasoning powers. But Jacob had never
yet so clearly understood as in this hour, why all
that was false, and why Abram had left Ur to
escape it. The vision vouchsafed him into this
immensity was full of horror but also of power;
his labour upon the godhead, which always
betrayed itself in his care-worn mien, made in
this awful night a progress not unconnected
with Rachel's agonies."

III

Volume two is the Book of Young Joseph, but
it is also still the book of Jacob, though there is a
lull in the vicissitudes of his life. The beauty and
promise of Rachel's son fill his days, — until there
occurs the great shock which arouses him again
to the old struggle to comprehend, in some measure, the dealings of God with man; to justify
God, as it were, and find some benign purpose
behind the brutality of accident and mischance.

The character of the relation between father
and son we have known ever since the long con-

versation between them on that spring night beside the well. There all Jacob's anxieties were at once revealed; his fear that the nature of the boy's gifts may lead him astray to admire the softer graces of other peoples, — their arts and sciences, which were irrelevant to a life for the Godhead, and should not concern the boy to whom he would undoubtedly give the " blessing." In short, the lad was already worldly, and with scant opportunity had managed to learn a great deal about other languages and other manners than those of his shepherd people. In this precocity Jacob sensed a danger. But he feared other dangers, — love can always see many. He is troubled to find the boy abroad at night, where a wild beast might fall upon him; a lion has been seen in the neighbourhood. And he is always ill at ease when the boy is near a well, a hole in the earth. Before Joseph's birth his grandfather, Laban, had consulted a heathen seer who foretold of the child Rachel carried that he should go down into a pit.

As for Joseph's attitude toward his father, it is what the good son's always will be. He loves Jacob because it is easy for him to love, respects him for all he has been and is, and pities him because his mind is shut against whatever is new and delightfully strange; against interesting languages and religions, against the clamour of founded cities and the customs of foreign peoples. He himself already knows a great deal more than Jacob, although he admits he is not so wise and has not been through so much.

When the second volume opens, Joseph is seventeen. He has learned many things since that night when he talked with Jacob by the well, but he is scarcely more mature. To pick up a new language easily, to astonish his father by his knowledge of tradition and the spiritual meaning of natural phenomena, to be the ornament and, indeed, the intellect, of his family; all this is quite enough to fill the days pleasantly at seventeen.

Very seldom does the personal charm of a character mysteriously reach out to one from the printed page. All authors claim it for their favourite creations, but their failure to make good their claim is so usual that we seldom stop to say to the writer: " But this is mere writing, I get no feeling of this person." For me, at least, Herr Mann wholly succeeds in communicating Joseph's highly individual charm. Mann's own consciousness of it is very strong, with something paternal in it, since he so often feels Joseph through Jacob's senses. When, only a few hours after its birth, Jacob first sees this baby which had seemed so unwilling to be born at all, when he regards the unusual shape and firmness of the head and the " strangely complete little hand," he knows that here is something different from all the other sturdy little animals which have been born to him. From that moment the reader also is able to believe in the special loveliness and equability and fine fibre of this child; here is no shepherd clod, but something that can take a high finish.

The misfortune of young Joseph is that he never meets with anything difficult enough to challenge his very unusual mind. What there is to be learned from his old teacher, and from the routine of a shepherds' camp, is mere child's play. Nothing very interesting ever happens now in Jacob's great family; so Joseph decorates the trivial events: he exaggerates, gossips, talks too much, and is extravagantly given to dreams. These are not the dreams of lassitude, nor are they sensual. They are violent, dizzy, — nightmares of grandeur. The qualities which are to make his great future are in him, potential realities, just as they were in Napoleon at seventeen; and they have nothing to grapple with.

It was this " something," this innate superiority in the boy himself, which the brothers hated even more than they hated the father's favourite: a deeper and more galling kind of jealousy. The story of Joseph and his brothers is not only forever repeated in literature, it forever repeats itself in life. The natural antagonism between the sane and commonplace, and the exceptional and inventive, is never so bitter as when it occurs in a family: and Joseph certainly did nothing to conciliate his stolid brethren. He insisted upon believing (he had to insist, for he was not vain to the point of stupidity) that all his family rejoiced in his good looks and brilliancy and general superiority. Was he not an ornament to them? It did not occur to him that families which lead self-respecting, simple, industrious lives are not pleased with or benefited by ornaments of this kind — which put them in a false position, indeed. The richness of his own fancy and vitality was quite enough for the youth. Upon this limitation in Joseph the author comments as follows:

" Indifference to the inner life of other human beings, ignorance of their feelings, display an entirely warped attitude toward real life, they give rise to a certain blindness. Since the days of Adam and Eve, since the time when one became two, nobody has been able to live without wanting to put himself in his neighbour's place and explore his situation, even while trying to see it objectively. Imagination, the art of divining the emotional life of others — in other words, sympathy — is not only commendable inasmuch as it breaks down the limitations of the ego; it is always an indispensable means of self-preservation. But of these rules Joseph knew nothing. His blissful self-confidence was like that of a spoilt child; it persuaded him, despite all evidence to the contrary, that everyone loved him, even more than themselves."

Joseph heeded no preliminary warnings; he was awakened from his agreeable self-satisfaction only by a shock so terrible that he barely survived it at all, and this awakening was followed by a long and hazardous servitude among a hostile people. Life put him to the test, to many tests, and proved him; he was one of those whom mischances enlighten and refine. Behind the bright promise in him there was the sound seed which would grow to its full measure under any circumstances and could not be circumvented. The world is always full of brilliant youth which fades into grey and embittered middle age: the first flowering takes everything. The great men are those who have developed slowly, or who have been able to survive the glamour of their early florescence and to go on learning from life. If we could

> *look into the seeds of time,*
> *And say which grain will grow and which will*
> *not,*

our hopes for young talent would be disappointed less often. Yet in that very mystery lies much of the fascination which gifted young people have for their elders. Kindly effort to shelter them from struggle with the hard facts of existence is often to take away the bread (or the lack of it) by which they grow, if the power of growth is in them. Perhaps if young Joseph had been sent into Egypt on a pension fund or a travelling scholarship the end might have been very different.

The manner in which he actually sets out for Egypt is a challenge to fate, certainly: disinherited, bruised in body, rocking on the camel of Ishmaelite merchants who have bought him as a slave. Thus he vanishes from the story. We do not know at what point in his adventures we are first to see him again in Mann's third volume, but we know that his father is not to see him again until there has been such a reversal of fortune as seldom happens — even in old legends, with the direct intervention of the gods. Though he is brought so low when he leaves us, his state is not utterly hopeless. The brothers have beaten the conceit and joy out of him; all his sunny youth he has left behind him in the pit, and he has come out into the world naked as when he was born, without father or family or friends, owning not even his own body. But he is going toward a country where, if he really possesses the lively intelligence Jacob and old Eliezer imputed to him, it will find plenty to work upon.

The book ends with Jacob, for however much the story is Joseph's, it is always Jacob's. He is the compass, the north star, the seeking mind behind events; he divines their hidden causes. He knows that even external accidents often have their roots, their true beginnings, in personal feeling. He accepts the evidence of the bloody coat and believes that Joseph was devoured by a boar or a lion, yet his glance at the brothers is always accusing. But for their hatred, the wild beast might not have come down upon Joseph.

Jacob is the understanding witness of the whole play, and we know, when we close the second volume, that he will live to behold the unimaginable conclusion in Egypt. This is one of the advantages of making a new story out of an old one which is a very part of the readers' consciousness. The course of destiny is already known and fixed for us, it is not some story-teller's make-believe (though for strangeness no reckless improviser could surpass this one). What we most love is not bizarre invention, but to have the old story brought home to us closer than ever before, enriched by all that the right man could draw from it and, by sympathetic insight, put into it. Shakespeare knew this fact very well, and the Greek dramatists long before him.

Herr Mann stresses Joseph's charm of person and address with good reason. They are stressed even in the highly condensed account in the Book of Genesis. They are, indeed, the subject of Joseph's story. Had the Ishmaelites not recognized very exceptional values in him, they would have sold him in any slave market. Being sure of special qualities in this piece of merchandise, they held him for a high purchaser and disposed of him to the Captain of Pharaoh's guard. He charmed Potiphar and, to his misfortune, Potiphar's wife. When he was thrown into a dungeon, his jailor gave him the management of the prison. When he was brought before Pharaoh, he was given the management of the kingdom.

He had come into Egypt a slave, born of a half-savage people whom the cultivated Egyptians despised, and he had been trained to an occupation they despised. We are told in Genesis that " every shepherd was an abomination to the Egyptians." (We are not told why: perhaps because the Egyptian cotton market was already an important thing in the world?) It is not easy to find a parallel situation: suppose that a Navajo Indian shepherd boy had been gathered up by the Spanish explorers and sold to one of the world-roving merchant ships from Saint-Malo. Suppose, further, that we find this red Indian boy at the age of thirty become the virtual ruler of France, a Richelieu or a Mazarin.

How much of his remarkable career Herr Mann will accredit to Joseph's aptness in worldly affairs (that quality of which old Jacob was so distrustful), and how much to his direct inheritance from Jacob, that "blessing" (never formally given) which he carried with him into a land of subtleties and highly organized social life, I wait with impatience to learn. I suspect that I shall still find the father mightier than the son, and more remarkable as an imaginative creation.

Jacob is the rod of measure. He saw the beginning, the new-born creature, and believed even then that this was the child of destiny. He knew Joseph before Joseph knew himself. When the "true son" disappeared into darkness at the dawn of his promise, it was Jacob, not Joseph, who bore the full weight of the catastrophe and tasted the bitterness of death. And he lived to see the beautiful conclusion; not the worldly triumph only, but the greatness of heart which could forgive wrongs so shameful and cruel. Had not Jacob been there to recognize and to foresee, to be destroyed by grief and raised up again, the story of Joseph would lose its highest value. Joseph is the brilliant actor in the scene, but Jacob is the mind which created the piece itself. His brooding spirit wraps the legend in a loftiness and grandeur which actual events can never, in themselves, possess. Take Jacob out of the history of Joseph, and it becomes simply the story of young genius; its cruel discipline, its ultimate triumph and worldly success. A story ever new and always gratifying, but one which never wakens the deep vibrations of the soul.

KATHERINE MANSFIELD

I

Late in the autumn of 1920, on my way home from Naples, I had a glimpse of Katherine Mansfield through the eyes of a fellow passenger. As I have quite forgotten his real name, I shall call him Mr. J—. He was a New Englander, about sixty-five years of age, I conjectured; long, lean, bronzed, clear blue eyes, not very talkative. His face, however, had a way of talking to itself. When he sat reading, or merely looking at the water, changes went over his thin lips and brown cheeks which betokened silent soliloquy; amusement, doubtful deliberation, very often a good-humoured kind of scorn, accompanied by an audible sniff which was not the result of a cold. His profession was the law, I gathered, though he seemed to know a great deal about mines and mining engineering. Early American history was his personal passion, Francis Parkman and Sir George Otto Trevelyan. Though in both writers he found inconsistencies, he referred to these not superciliously but rather affectionately.

The voyage was very rough (we were delayed three days by bad weather), the cabin passengers were few and the wind and cold kept most of them in their staterooms. I found Mr. J— good company. He wore well. Though I have forgotten his name, I have not forgotten him. He was an original, a queer stick, intelligent but whimsical and crochety, quickly prejudiced for or against people by trifling mannerisms. He dined alone at a small table and always dressed for dinner though no one else did.

He was an agreeable companion chiefly because

he was so unexpected. For example: one morning when he was muttering dry witticisms about the boat's having lost so much time, he threw off carelessly that he was trying to get home for his mother's *ninetieth* birthday celebration, " though we are not on good terms, by any means," he chuckled.

I said I had supposed that family differences were outlawed at ninety.

" Not in our family," he brought out with relish.

He was a true chip, and proud of the old block. He was bringing a present home to her — a great bundle of leopard skins, which he showed to me. (He had lately been in Africa.)

He was a bachelor, of course, but when we were filling out declarations for customs, he had a number of expensive toys to declare (besides the leopard skins) and sport clothes for young men. Nephews, I asked? Not altogether, with a twist of the face. Some of his old friends had done him the compliment of naming sons after him. Yes, I thought, a bachelor of this kidney was just the man who would be welcome in other men's homes; he would be a cheerful interruption in the domestic monotony of correct, sound people like himself. Possibly he would have friends among people very unlike himself.

One afternoon as he sat down in his deck chair he picked up a volume of Synge's plays lying on my rug. He looked at it and observed:

" Trevelyan is the one English writer I would really like to meet. The old man."

He glanced through my book for a few moments, then put it back on my knee and asked abruptly: " What do you think of Katherine Mansfield? "

I told him I had read her very little (English friends had sent me over a story of hers from time to time), but I thought her very talented.

" You think so, do you." It was not a question, but a verdict, delivered in his driest manner, with a slight sniff. After a moment he said he had letters to write and went away. Why a specialist in the American Revolution and the French and Indian wars should ask me about a girl then scarcely heard of in America, and why he should be displeased at my answer —

The next morning I saw him doing his usual half-hour on the deck. " Climbing the deck," he called it, because now, in addition to the inconveniences of rough weather, we had a very bad list. Mr. J— explained that it came about because the coal hadn't been properly trimmed and had shifted. Very dangerous with a heavy sea every day . . . disgrace to seamanship . . . couldn't have happened on a British steamer . . . Italians and French in the engine room. After climbing and descending the deck until he had satisfied his conscience, he sat down beside me and flapped his rug over his knees.

" The young lady we were speaking of yesterday: she writes under a *nom de plume*. Her true name is not Mansfield, but Beauchamp."

" That I didn't know. I know nothing about her, really."

He relapsed into one of his long silences, and I went on reading.

" May I send the deck steward to my cabin for

some sherry, instead of that logwood he would bring us from the bar? "

The sherry appeared. After we had drunk a few glasses, Mr. J— began: " The young lady we were speaking of; I happen to have seen her several times, though I certainly don't move in literary circles."

I expressed surprise and interest, but he did not go on at once. He sent the steward for more biscuit, and got up to test the lashings of his deck chair and mine. We were on the port side where the wind was milder but the list was worse. At last he made himself comfortable and began to tell me that he had once gone out to Australia and New Zealand on business matters. He was very specific as to dates, geography, boat and railway connections. He elaborated upon these details. I suppose because they were safe and sane, things you could check up on, while the real subject of his communication proved to be very vague. I did not listen attentively; I had only the dimmest conception of those distant British colonies. He was telling me about a boat trip he had made from New Zealand to some Australian port, when gradually his manner changed; he rambled and was more wary. As he became more cautious I became more interested. I wish I could repeat his story exactly as he told it, but his way of talking was peculiar to himself and I can only give the outline:

Among the people who were coming on board his steamer when he left New Zealand, Mr. J— noticed a family party: several children, a man who was evidently their father, and an old lady who seemed of quite a different class than the other passengers. She was quiet, gentle, had the children perfectly under control. She conducted them below as soon as the boat took off. When they reappeared on deck they had changed their shore things for play clothes. Mr. J— remembered very little about the father, " the usual pushing colonial type," but he distinctly remembered the old lady, and a little girl with thin legs and large eyes who wandered away from the family and apparently wished to explore the steamer for herself. Presently she came and sat down next Mr. J—, which pleased him. She was shy, but so happy to be going on a journey that she answered his questions and talked to him as if he were not a stranger. She was delighted with everything; the boat, the water, the weather, the gulls which followed the steamer. " But have you ever seen them *eat?* " she asked. " That is terrible! "

The next morning Mr. J— was up and out very early; found the deck washed down and empty. But up in the bow he saw his little friend of yesterday, doing some sort of gymnastic exercises, " quick as a bird." He joined her and asked if she had breakfasted. No, she was waiting for the others.

" Mustn't exercise too much before breakfast," he told her. " Come and sit down with me." As they walked toward his chair he noticed that she had put on a fresh dress for the morning. Mr. J— said it was " embroidered " (probably cross-stitched) with yellow ducks, all in a row round the hem. He complimented her upon the ducks.

" I thought they would astonish you," she said complacently.

As they sat and talked she kept smoothing her skirt and settling her sleeves, which had a duck on each cuff. Something pleased Mr. J— very much as he recalled the little girl, and her satisfaction with her fresh dress on that fresh morning aboard a little coasting steamer. His eyes twinkled and he chuckled. " She adopted me for the rest of the voyage," he concluded.

No, he couldn't say exactly what the charm of the child was. She struck him as intensely alert, with a deep curiosity altogether different from the flighty, excited curiosity usual in children. She turned things over in her head and asked him questions which surprised him. She was sometimes with her grandmother and the other children, but oftener alone, going about the boat, looking the world over with quiet satisfaction. When she was with him, he did not talk to her a great deal, because he liked better to watch her " taking it all in." It was on her account he had always remembered that short trip, out of many boat trips. She told him her name, and he easily remembered it " because of *Beauchamp's Career,* you see."

" And now do you want chapter two? " Mr. J— asked me. He twisted his face and rubbed his chin.

A few years ago he had been in London on a confidential mission for a client who was also an old friend. The nature of his business took him more or less among people not of his kind and not especially to his liking. (He paused here as if taking counsel with his discretion, and I wondered whether we were to have another version of Henry James' *The Ambassadors.*) In the places frequented by this uncongenial " circle " he heard talk of a girl from New Zealand who " could knock the standard British authors into a cocked hat," though she didn't very easily find a publisher. She scorned conventions, and had got herself talked about. He heard her name spoken. There could be no doubt; from the same part of the world, and the name he had never forgotten. The young lady herself was pointed out to him once in a restaurant, by the young man whose affairs he had come over to manage. She was just back from the Continent, and her friends were giving a dinner for her. As he expected; the same face, the same eyes. She did not fit the gossip he had been hearing; quite the contrary. She looked to him almost demure, — except for something challenging in her eyes, perhaps. And she seemed very frail. He felt a strong inclination to look her up. He decided to write to her, but he thought he had better inform himself a little first. He asked his client whether he had anything Miss Mansfield had written. The young man, doubtless with humorous intent, produced a pamphlet which had been privately printed: *Je ne parle pas français.* After reading it, Mr. J— felt there would be no point in meeting the young writer. He saw her once afterward, at the theatre. When the play was on and the lights were down, she looked, he thought, ill and unhappy. He heartily wished he had never seen or heard of her since that boat trip.

Mr. J— turned to me sharply: " *Je ne parle pas*

français — and what do you think of that story, may I ask? "

I had not read it.

" Well, I have. I didn't dismiss it lightly; artificial, and unpleasantly hysterical, full of affectations; she had none as a child." He spoke rather bitterly: his disappointment was genuine.

II

Every writer and critic of discernment who looked into Katherine Mansfield's first volume of short stories must have felt that here was a very individual talent. At this particular time few writers care much about their medium except as a means for expressing ideas. But in Katherine Mansfield one recognized virtuosity, a love for the medium she had chosen.

The qualities of a second-rate writer can easily be defined, but a first-rate writer can only be experienced. It is just the thing in him which escapes analysis that makes him first-rate. One can catalogue all the qualities that he shares with other writers, but the thing that is his very own, his timbre, this cannot be defined or explained any more than the quality of a beautiful speaking voice can be.

It was usually Miss Mansfield's way to approach the major forces of life through comparatively trivial incidents. She chose a small reflector to throw a luminous streak out into the shadowy realm of personal relationships. I feel that personal relationships, especially the uncatalogued ones, the seemingly unimportant ones, interested her most. To my thinking, she never measured herself up so fully as in the two remarkable stories about an English family in New Zealand, " Prelude " and " At the Bay."

I doubt whether any contemporary writer has made one feel more keenly the many kinds of personal relations which exist in an everyday " happy family " who are merely going on living their daily lives, with no crises or shocks or bewildering complications to try them. Yet every individual in that household (even the children) is clinging passionately to his individual soul, is in terror of losing it in the general family flavour. As in most families, the mere struggle to have anything of one's own, to be one's self at all, creates an element of strain which keeps everybody almost at the breaking-point.

One realizes that even in harmonious families there is this double life: the group life, which is the one we can observe in our neighbour's household, and, underneath, another — secret and passionate and intense — which is the real life that stamps the faces and gives character to the voices of our friends. Always in his mind each member of these social units is escaping, running away, trying to break the net which circumstances and his own affections have woven about him. One realizes that human relationships are the tragic necessity of human life; that they can never be wholly satisfactory, that every ego is half the time greedily seeking them, and half the time pulling away from them. In those simple relationships of loving husband and wife, affectionate sisters, children and grandmother, there are innumerable shades of sweetness and anguish which make up the pattern of our lives day by day, though they are not down in the list of subjects from which the conventional novelist works.

Katherine Mansfield's peculiar gift lay in her interpretation of these secret accords and antipathies which lie hidden under our everyday behaviour, and which more than any outward events make our lives happy or unhappy. Had she lived, her development would have gone on in this direction more than in any other. When she touches this New Zealand family and those far-away memories ever so lightly, as in " The Doll's House," there is a magic one does not find in the other stories, fine as some of them are. With this theme the very letters on the page become alive. She communicates vastly more than she actually writes. One goes back and runs through the pages to find the text which made one know certain things about Linda or Burnell or Beryl, and the text is not there — but something was there, all the same — is there, though no typesetter will ever set it. It is this overtone, which is too fine for the printing press and comes through without it, that makes one know that this writer had something of the gift which is one of the rarest things in writing, and quite the most precious. That she had not the happiness of developing her powers to the full, is sad enough. She wrote the truth from Fontainebleau a few weeks before she died: "*The old mechanism isn't mine any longer, and I can't control the new.*" She had lived through the first stage, had outgrown her young art, so that it seemed false to her in comparison with the new light that was breaking within. The "new mechanism," big enough to convey the new knowledge, she had not the bodily strength to set in motion.

III

Katherine Mansfield's published *Journal* begins in 1914 and ends in 1922, some months before her death. It is the record of a long struggle with illness, made more cruel by lack of money and by the physical hardships that war conditions brought about in England and France. At the age of twenty-two (when most young people have a secret conviction that they are immortal), she was already ill in a Bavarian *pension*. From the time when she left New Zealand and came back to England to make her own way, there was never an interval in which she did not have to drive herself beyond her strength. She never reached the stage when she could work with a relaxed elbow. In her story " Prelude," when the family are moving, and the storeman lifts the little girl into the dray and tucks her up, he says: " Easy does it." She knew this, long afterward, but she never had a chance to put that method into practice. In all her earlier stories there is something fierce about her attack, as if she took up a new tale in the spirit of overcoming it. " Do or die " is the mood, — indeed, she must have faced that alternative more than once: a girl come back to make her living in London, without health or money or influential friends, — with no assets but talent and pride.

In her volume of stories entitled *Bliss*, published in 1920 (most of them had been written some years before and had appeared in periodicals), she throws down her glove, utters her little challenge in the high language which she knew better than did most of her readers:

> *But I tell you, my lord fool, out of this nettle, danger, we pluck this flower, safety.*

A fine attitude, youthful and fiery: out of all the difficulties of life and art we will snatch *something*. No one was ever less afraid of the nettle; she was defrauded unfairly of the physical vigour which seems the natural accompaniment of a high and daring spirit.

At thirteen Katherine Mansfield made the long voyage to England with her grandmother, to go to school in London. At eighteen she returned to her own family in Wellington, New Zealand. It was then the struggle against circumstances began. She afterward burned all her early diaries, but it is those I should have liked to read. Exile may be easy to bear for those who have lived their lives. But at eighteen, after four years of London, to be thrown back into a prosperous commercial colony at the end of the world, was starvation. There is no homesickness and no hunger so unbearable. Many a young artist would sell his future, all his chances, simply to get back to the world where other people are doing the only things that, to his inexperience, seem worth doing at all.

Years afterward, when Katherine Mansfield had begun to do her best work but was rapidly sinking in vitality, her homesickness stretched all the other way — backwards, for New Zealand and that same crude Wellington. Unpromising as it was for her purpose, she felt that it was the only territory she could claim, in the deepest sense, as her own. The *Journal* tells us how often she went back to it in her sleep. She recounts these dreams at some length: but the entry which makes one realize that homesickness most keenly is a short one, made in Cornwall in 1918:

" *June 20th.* The twentieth of June 1918.
C'est de la misère.

Non, pas ça exactement. Il y a quelque chose — une profonde malaise me suive comme un ombre.

Oh, why write bad French? Why write at all? 11,500 miles are so many — too many by 11,499¾ for me."

Eleven thousand five hundred miles is the distance from England to New Zealand.

By this, 1918, she had served her apprenticeship. She had gone through a succession of enthusiasms for this master and that, formed friendships with some of the young writers of her own time. But the person who had freed her from the self-consciousness and affectations of the experimenting young writer, and had brought her to her realest self, was not one of her literary friends but, quite simply, her own brother.

He came over in 1915 to serve as an officer. He was younger than she, and she had not seen him for six years. After a short visit with her in London he went to the front, and a few weeks later was killed in action. But he had brought to his sister the New Zealand of their childhood, and out of those memories her best stories were to grow. For the remaining seven years of her life (she died just under thirty-five) her brother seems to have been almost constantly in her mind. A great change comes over her feelings about art; what it is, and why it is. When she prays to become "humble," it is probably the slightly showy quality in the early stories that she begs to be delivered from — and forgiven for. The *Journal* from 1918 on is a record of a readjustment to life, a changing sense of its deepest realities. One of the entries in 1919 recounts a dream in which her brother, "Chummie," came back to her:

> "I hear his hat and stick thrown on to the hall-table. He runs up the stairs, three at a time. 'Hullo, darling!' But I can't move — I can't move. He puts his arm round me, holding me tightly, and we kiss — a long, firm, family kiss. And the kiss means: We are of the same blood; we have absolute confidence in each other; we love; all is well; nothing can ever come between us."

In the same year she writes:

" Now it is May 1919. Six o'clock. I am sitting in my own room thinking of Mother: I want to cry. But my thoughts are beautiful and full of gaiety. I think of *our* house, *our* garden, *us* children — the lawn, the gate, and Mother coming in. ' Children! Children! ' I really only ask for time to write it all."

But she did not find too late the things she cared for most. She could not have written that group of New Zealand stories when she first came to London. There had to be a long period of writing for writing's sake. The spontaneous untutored outpouring of personal feeling does not go very far in art. It is only the practised hand that can make the natural gesture, — and the practised hand has often to grope its way. She tells us that she made four false starts on " At the Bay," and when she finished the story it took her nearly a month to recover.

The *Journal*, painful though it is to read, is not the story of utter defeat. She had not, as she said, the physical strength to write what she now knew were, to her, the most important things in life. But she had found them, she possessed them, her mind fed on them. On them, and on the language of her greatest poet. (She read Shakespeare continually, when she was too ill to leave her bed.) The inexhaustible richness of that language seems to have been like a powerful cordial, warmed her when bodily nourishment failed her.

Among the stories she left unfinished there is one of singular beauty, written in the autumn of 1922, a few months before her death, the last piece of work she did. She called it " Six Years After ": Linda and Burnell grown old, and the boy six years dead. It has the same powerful slightness which distinguishes the other New Zealand stories, and an even deeper tenderness.

Of the first of the New Zealand stories, " Prelude," Miss Mansfield wrote in answer to the inquiries of an intimate friend:

" This is about as much as I can say about it. You know, if the truth were known, I have a perfect passion for the island where I was born. Well, in the early morning there I always remember feeling that this little island has dipped back into the dark blue sea during the night only to rise again at gleam of day, all hung with bright spangles and glittering drops. (When you ran over the dewy grass you positively felt that your feet tasted salt.) I tried to catch that moment — with something of its sparkle and its flavour. And just as on those mornings white milky mists rise and uncover some beauty, then smother it again and then again disclose it, I tried to lift that mist from my people and let them be seen and then to hide them again. . . . It's so difficult to describe all this and it sounds perhaps over-ambitious and vain."

An unpretentious but very suggestive statement of how an artist sets to work, and of the hazy sort of thing that almost surely lies behind and directs interesting or beautiful design. And not with the slighter talents only. Tolstoi him-

Katherine Mansfield

self, one knows from the different Lives and letters, went to work in very much the same way.
The long novels, as well as the short tales, grew
out of little family dramas, personal intolerances
and predilections, — promptings not apparent to
the casual reader and incomprehensible to the
commercial novel-maker.